no mountain
too high

no mountain too high

A Father's Inspiring
Journey Through Grief

NED LEVITT

ECW PRESS
ecwpress.com

Published by ECW Press
2120 Queen Street, Suite 200, Toronto, Ontario, Canada M4E 1E2

National Library of Canada Cataloguing in Publication

Levitt, Ned
No Mountain Too High –
A Father's Inspiring Journey Through Grief
ISBN 1-55022-672-X

1. Inspirational   2. Self-improvement   3. Memoir

Design and Page Formatting: PageWave Graphics Inc.
Cover Photo: Little Dog Productions Inc.
Printing: Transcontinental Best Book

The publication of *No Mountain Too High* has been generously supported by The Canada Council, the Ontario Arts Council, and the Government of Canada through the Book Publishing Industry Development Program.

Distribution
Canada: Jaguar Book Group, 100 Armstrong Avenue,
Georgetown, ON L5G 5S4

United States: Independent Publishers Group,
814 North Franklin Street, Chicago, Illinois 60610

Printed and Bound in Canada

To Stacey

contents

preface

NOTHING IN LIFE PREPARES YOU FOR THE DEATH OF YOUR CHILD. When it happens, you begin a struggle first to survive, then to preserve your relationships, and then to live, not just exist. No one can heal you; the healing must come from within. Relationships, whether they be with family or friends, are the soil in which you plant the seeds of hope and in which your new life takes root and grows. I owe a debt to all those wonderful people who helped me in so many ways, often without their even knowing, to beat back the demons and allow a new life to grow without Stacey's physical presence.

At the time of writing this preface it has been eight years, five months, fifteen days, nineteen hours, and twenty-seven minutes since Stacey died, on August 30, 1995. This book recounts many of the significant milestones and extraordinary events that have characterized my life and journey since that fateful day. It is my story and my view of the events that have had an impact on me and my family. The other members of the family may, as one would expect, have different recollections and views of the same events.

Obviously, this book would never have been written if Stacey had not died. But it is also true that this book would not have been written had she not written her poetry and had she not possessed such an extraordinary passion for life. Most of all, this book would never have been written if I did not love her beyond all comprehension and human capacity to love.

Only one other person shares this pain equally with me, and that is my wife, Cheryl. We gave Stacey life and never imagined that we would have to live without her. The odds of a marriage surviving the death of a child are dismal. Ours has, and this is due as much to our unfailing respect for each other as to our deep and abiding love. We are very different people in many ways, and I want to thank her from the deepest part of who I am for letting me grieve Stacey in my own unique and public way.

One thing that irks me is when people say, "But you do have two other daughters." My daughters are not interchangeable parts that can be moved into place when one part disappears. Each of Marni, Stacey, and Jacqueline has her own unique and special place in my heart. Would I miss my sight more than my hearing? Would I miss my right leg more than my left? Would I give up the sense of taste or the ability to feel love if I had to choose one? I love Marni and Jacqueline with the same depth and intensity that I love Stacey, and I want them to know how grateful I am to them for letting me do what I had to do to grieve Stacey, even as they needed me. Their love and support was and is crucial to me and they never let me down, even as they struggled with their own grief.

This book would never have been attempted if it were not for the foresight, expertise, and encouragement of Arnold Gosewich. He has lived and breathed books for a lifetime and saw in my journey a story that could and should be told in print. I am eternally grateful to him for his insight, patience, and determination.

CHAPTER ONE

the end

Death is not evil with devils,
nor kind with angels.
It is simply me
taking you in
so you can fight through another life
FROM "ENCOUNTER WITH DEATH," STACEY LEVITT, 1989

MY EYES OPENED AT 5:51 A.M., NINE MINUTES BEFORE THE clock radio was set to wake me with the breaking news of the day.

"It's another beautiful summer day in Toronto," the broadcaster informed me jovially. "We're expecting sunshine all day long."

It was a Wednesday in August, and we had come to expect such days as a right, following months of warm, sunny weather, reminiscent of my boyhood summers at Thunder Beach, in cottage country north of the city.

The morning fog of sleep lifted quickly, and I moved smoothly through my early morning rituals. With each small task accomplished, my enthusiasm for the day increased. After a twenty-minute drive downtown, I entered the Plaza Club, close to my office, and floated through my workout with ease: a varied combination of aerobics, weight training, and stretching. Throughout that summer, I had been outside a lot, spending many weekends cycling, windsurfing, and playing tennis at Thunder Beach. Inevitably, I feel healthier and in better shape at the end of summer than at any other time of the year: a consequence of living in Canada, a country that tortures its citizens for months on end with cold and darkness and confinement to basement recreation rooms.

After a short walk to my law office in the Scotia Plaza, my work day began. I looked at my schedule. It was going to be a day filled with lots of interesting and varied work activities, not the least of which would be my attendance at the Ministry of Consumer and Commercial Relations offices at the north end of Toronto's mammoth shopping mall, the Eaton Centre, to sign the final report of the Franchise Sector Working Team. This would cap years of meetings, study, and debate about the future of franchise legislation in Ontario.

It had been more than twenty years since I started practicing law. Even as an articling student, I had been captivated by franchise law. Back in the mid-1970s, it was new and not well known — in fact, I had found it difficult, in my articling year, to track down resources to complete the assignments given to me in this area. I was fortunate to have had an instinct that franchise law was bound to grow in Canada. Now, it had become almost mainstream, and I had built a thriving practice specializing in it.

I had never before been part of a legislative process. It thrilled me to sign my name to such an important document. As I did, I took note of the date, August 30, 1995, a date that I knew would be referred to frequently as the legislative process unfolded.

We were more than halfway through the second year of our new firm, Levitt, Beber, and the extraordinary success we experienced right from the start was holding. I had run my own small law firm for the majority of my career, but, in the merger frenzy of the late 1980s, events conspired to lead me, in 1990, to merge my small firm with a much larger one. From the very beginning of the merger, I was a fish out of water. I spent two years trying to make it work and two years planning my exit. On February 1, 1994, I left with one partner and several associates and returned to what I knew best and felt most comfortable with, my own small firm. The mood around the office was upbeat and optimistic. The future looked good.

It was 7:00 p.m. when the last of the franchisees arrived for a meeting with me at my office. I heard the usual complaint about a franchisor who was more interested in his profits than theirs. After we hashed out an action plan for these clients, we wrapped the meeting up, at around 9:15 p.m. I headed home, tired but satisfied with a day well spent.

At that hour, the traffic was light and it was clear and warm. I opened the sun roof and every window in my car to feel the evening air. I glanced up at the bright stars against the black night sky and took note of what a lovely late summer's evening it was. I began to unwind.

About halfway to my home, in the central part of the city, I called my eldest daughter, Marni, in Montreal, where she was starting another year at McGill University. The conversation was unusually long and pleasant, one of those rare moments, especially when your children are entering adulthood, when you feel really connected.

I live in a Tudor style home that was built in the 1930s. The garage is small and serves only as a storage shed. I eased the car into the driveway and entered the house. My wife, Cheryl, and our youngest daughter, Jacqueline, had just returned from shopping at Yorkdale Plaza. Stacey, the middle of our three daughters, had been shopping for clothes that day for the new school year and had laid all of her purchases out neatly on her bed to show everyone. Gone were the bright colors and glitz of her childhood clothing, replaced by stylish simplicity and earth tones. Stacey knew what she wanted in clothing and no one was invited along on her shopping trips. As far as anyone knew, Stacey was out having dinner with her friend Amy.

As I began to unwind that evening, safe in the warmth of my home, I thought of how proud I was to be the father of such fine young women as Marni, Stacey, and Jacqueline, each of them so different, yet all of them so loving of Cheryl and me, and of each other. At this time Marni was twenty, Stacey, eighteen, and Jacqueline, sixteen.

Marni, our firstborn, was always the most cerebral. She could enjoy herself, but more often was serious and intense. While she was still in her crib, I would sit cross-legged on the floor and say, "Let's have a talk." She would join in with gibberish, which sounded like conversation even if neither of us knew what she was saying. She shared my love of the outdoors, and we enjoyed many a long bike ride, jog, or ski day together, always filled with stimulating conversation. She took to music at an early age and discovered a talent for song-writing and performing. Marni holds tightly to her independence and finds great satisfaction in living life in her own way and on her own terms.

Jacquie is my twin, both in looks and temperament. Our clashes are renowned, and so is our love for each other. I did, however, have the pleasure, along with Cheryl, of literally wringing her neck every day during her first year. It was on doctor's orders because she had a shortened neck muscle that needed physiotherapy. To this day she has been trying to get even with us for those early ministrations. Jacquie has the proverbial steel-trap mind and an innate sense of business. Without breaking a sweat, she could negotiate the best allowance and justify taking not only her share of whatever, but her sisters' as well.

Stacey, more than her sisters, wanted to do what I did and wanted to learn what I knew. She excelled at learning sports. She loved to learn, and I loved to teach. I overcame my claustrophobia to learn scuba diving, because Stacey wanted to try it. For some reason, when she was with me, I felt safe underwater.

I once asked Marni and Jacqueline if it bothered them that Stacey and I did so many activities together. "Are you kidding?" Jacqueline said. "We're happy you do. It means she uses up your energy and you leave us alone!"

Stacey was, from the very beginning, a happy and outgoing child. I was certain, when she was only weeks old, that she was smiling. The experts said it was only gas. At only a few months of age her arms would shoot up to receive me like they were spring-loaded. She loved nothing more than to be held and touched.

It seems that each child has a different father. Stacey's father was older and calmer than Marni's father, because I had already worked out some of my anxieties about being responsible for another's existence by the time she arrived on the scene. This may explain why second-borns often seem so much more easygoing and adventurous.

Stacey's eyes were happy blue, her hair was the color of wheat, and she had dimples that were deep and inviting. She was beautiful on the inside and on the outside. She charmed you before you realized it. People felt good around her, without really knowing why. I gradually figured out her secret: she made everyone feel good about themselves. Subtly, she made you feel that your story was the most interesting thing she had ever heard. She was genuinely interested in people and their experiences.

I remember what I said at Stacey's Bat Mitzvah, the service commemorating her reaching the age of thirteen and taking her place, religiously, as an adult in the Jewish community: "If you have ever caressed a cloud, hugged a rainbow, or kissed a sunbeam, you would know what it is like to be Stacey's father." In the years that followed that occasion, Stacey grew into a beautiful young woman, with strength of body and character. She had an incredible zest for life. We showered her with love, and she seemed to take it in as fuel, process it, and love us back times two.

With three daughters two years apart from each other, our house was, to say the least, busy. I remember nights when all three had colds and I would take my turn tending to their needs. I raced from Marni's room, to Stacey's room, to Jacqueline's room, and then back to Marni's room, to begin the circuit again, getting drinks, applying cold washcloths to foreheads, and administering medicine. It made me feel like the circus performer keeping a large number of plates spinning on a line of thin poles by racing to each plate, in turn, as it starts to lose momentum and re-energizing it just before it crashes to the floor.

Reading to the girls was a nightly ritual for Cheryl and me. *Alligator Pie*, *Goodnight Moon*, and the Robert Munsch books were some of their favorites. Sometimes I told them stories of my adventures as a boy with my brother, Frank.

I also loved to make up games for them and me to play. One was Hide the People, played with many small Sesame Street characters hidden by me and found by them in a darkened room with flashlights. Another was Swing Ball, in which they would try to kick the soccer ball I threw to them while they were swinging as high as they could on the swing set in our back yard. My favorite was a self-serving game I called the Kissing Game. I would lie on the bed and Marni, Jacqueline, and Stacey would sit one on my left, another on my right, and the third on my stomach. Then I would call out, "Who can give me the _____ kiss?" In turn, the blank was filled in by "wettest," "driest," "softest," "smoothest," "quickest, "meanest," "happiest," "saddest," "nicest," "loudest," "quietest," or "sweetest." They would then, in turn, plant the appropriate kiss, with sound effects, on one of my cheeks. After each round, I would choose a winner. It was amazing how many times these games ended in a three-way tie.

Cheryl made sure that the girl's imaginations were always nourished. She took them to arts groups, play groups, dance lessons, music lessons, rhythmic gymnastic classes, and more. Creative expression was always encouraged. However, one evening I realized that we may have gone too far. On arriving home, I was greeted by Cheryl yelling, "The girls are nuts!"

Bracing myself for the latest catastrophe, I asked, "What happened now?"

Cheryl answered in an exasperated tone, "I looked out

the window just after school and there they were, stark naked, hanging from the swing set, peeing like baboons!"

I had my work cut out for me being the only male in our household. (Even when a puppy was chosen for the family, it was a female one. I was always outvoted.) Mealtimes were tumultuous and challenging. I always listened to the weather reports in the morning to decide how to dress for the weekdays for work or for the weekends for whatever sports we were planning to do. I wish there had also been a mood forecast, to help me prepare for the climate in my home each day. When the girls were teenagers, I needed a machete to cut through the hormones just to get into my house after work.

All this basking in what seemed a perfect day at work and at home was interrupted dramatically around 10 p.m.

"Dad, Mom, something's wrong," Jacqueline yelled, running up the stairs from the recreation room into the kitchen, where Cheryl and I were sitting. She could hardly get the words out. "A policeman just called asking for Stacey," she said. She was obviously trying to stay in control. "He asked me to describe her and wanted to know if she had any distinguishing marks. I told him about the tattoo of a dolphin on her ankle." She took a long pause and then added, "He said that a young woman matching that description was hit by a car and was at Sunnybrook Hospital. He's coming over to see us."

We kept going over and over the limited facts we had. We moved from the kitchen, down the hall to the living room, then back again, then into the dining room and back to the kitchen. Cheryl kept asking what we should do. I tried to move to the place inside me where I had always escaped as a child when chaos overtook my world. Cheryl had the good sense to call our close friends Saul and Mirna Alter, who rushed over immediately.

I kept calling the police station and then the hospital to get information, but no one would tell me anything. I don't know why I did not just get in my car and go to the hospital. I kept stepping out the front door and peering down the street in each direction, then up at the night sky, at the same stars I had seen through such different eyes less than two hours before.

The policeman took about half an hour to arrive. He parked his black-and-white cruiser half on our driveway and half on the road, angled the way the police do when they are in a hurry to do their duty. He was big, at least six feet two inches tall, fully equipped with gun, handcuffs, and nightstick hanging from his belt. He looked completely out of place in our living room.

The officer wasted no time. He asked to see a picture of Stacey. Jacqueline escorted him across our living room and showed him a picture we had of her along with pictures of the other girls on a cabinet that housed our television. Ill at ease, but determined to do what he knew he had to do, he informed us that a young woman matching Stacey's description, who had been out jogging, had been hit by a car at Ledbury and Lawrence, and had succumbed to her injuries.

"Had succumbed to her injuries?" The words bounced around in my head like a pinball. I could not comprehend the meaning of the words. Stacey could not be dead. I knew my parents would die one day. My father was in fact close to death. I knew I would die eventually, though I harbored some hope that I wouldn't. But Stacey, my child, my future, my legacy, my kadishila, was immortal. Immortal to me, for all intents and purposes, because I would not be on earth to witness her death. How could someone who is immortal die?

Chaos was then unleashed in our home. Cheryl broke down, screaming, "No, no, no," over and over again, crying and pounding her fist on every surface close to her. She could not be consoled. Jacquie just sat still, stunned. I looked from one to the other, back and forth, and then at the policeman, as if he could put an end to the whole scene.

The policeman somehow stayed calm through all of this. He said we should go to the hospital. I walked out of the house and stepped into the front seat of his cruiser. Jacqueline slipped into the back seat. Cheryl followed in Saul's car with Mirna. As we drove along, the radio crackled with the sounds of police business in the city. Between the waves of nausea that were washing over me, I wondered what this guy was thinking. How hard was this for him? Did he have children himself? How many times had he had to do this? We seemed to have an understanding. I did not ask any questions, and he did not offer any more information.

It was now about 11 p.m. We pulled into Sunnybrook Hospital, a short distance from our home. I was ushered into the emergency department like a VIP, but no one was rushing up for an autograph. In fact, I had the distinct impression that nobody wanted to get too close to me, as if I had a contagious and deadly disease. The look in the eyes of the nurses, as I walked in, took away the last bit of hope, to which I was clinging for sanity, that Stacey was still alive.

One nurse pointed to a door and said that I should go in there and tell them if it was Stacey. She warned me that I would see tubes in her mouth and that she had sustained severe head injuries. I asked Jacqueline if she wanted to come with me. She just shook her head no. Saul moved to be beside me. It was fitting that he was with me at that moment. His youngest daughter, Lori, and Stacey were the closest of friends. Our families vacationed together and celebrated holidays and life events together almost like one family. In fact, Stacey and Lori were born on the same day, at the same hospital, and Cheryl and Saul's wife, Mirna, were even in the same hospital room. The families' friendship started, however, by chance, when we moved onto their street several years later.

The door was hospital beige, metal, and huge. It inched open, as if in some B horror movie. Time slowed and everything began to stretch out in slow motion. The room itself was cavernous, or so it seemed. There was a great deal of medical equipment and at least two people in hospital attire.

I had to force myself to look across the room at the operating table. There, stretched out as if she was sleeping, was my Stacey. I had a sick feeling in the pit of my stomach. The staff had ensured that I would view her right side as I entered the room — the fatal damage was to the left side of her head. I saw that they had taken her trademark long, curly blonde hair and arranged it as a cover to the injuries.

I stayed back about ten or twelve feet. I was incapable of going any closer. I screamed, "Oh, noooo…," and then began to weep. Finally, after several minutes, I asked the nurse if I could come back later. The answer was yes, but I never returned, perhaps out of the fear of death itself, the need to help Cheryl and Jacqueline, or simply the need to distance myself from the pain.

I was reared in an emotionally chaotic home and developed a defense mechanism that makes me calmer as those around me become more agitated and my environment more dangerous. Cheryl and Jacqueline had discovered from my scream the awful truth that Stacey was indeed gone. They could not contain themselves. As the chaos in the emergency ward deepened, with other patients and families needing attention from the staff, I began methodically making phone calls from a phone just outside the hospital's "quiet room," a peculiar name for a room from which now emanated the howlings of a bereaved mother and sister. I have always understood this to be a room where people are sent to shut out the hustle and bustle of the hospital while they dealt with their "issues." I discovered that night that there is another purpose for this room: protecting the rest of the hospital from being disturbed by the wrenching sounds of human emotions as family and friends try to cope with the cruelties of life. The room was sparsely decorated in a sort of "early bowling alley" motif. It was too small to contain the ocean of grief pouring from all of us.

My first phone call was to Rabbi Dolgin, the associate rabbi of our synagogue, Temple Sinai.

"Hello, Rabbi… I am sorry to disturb you so late," I said calmly. "Stacey is dead."

What did I just say? "Stacey is dead"? I did not believe what I was saying. I was simply repeating what I was told by the people around me. My rabbi was silent for a moment as he absorbed this shocking news.

"How are Cheryl and Jacqueline?" he asked.

"Not doing so well," I answered.

"Do your parents know?" I had not thought about them until he asked that question. We both knew how sick my father was and I wondered how they would take this news and how I would tell them. Before I could utter the words,

the rabbi said, "I will go to your parents now and tell them."
I felt a flash of relief and thanked him.

The next phone call was to Marni. How was I to tell my
daughter that her beloved sister had been hit by a car and
died? Should I concoct a story to get her to fly immediately
from Montreal and then tell her as she walked off the plane?
I was in no shape to come up with a believable lie, nor
would someone as intelligent as she believe it. There really
was no choice.

"Marni ... Stacey was jogging and got hit by a car. She is
dead." I heard her gasp. She said nothing.

"You need to get home as soon as possible, Marni."

"I will. How are Mom and Jacqueline?" she asked.

"Not doing so well."

A man had been standing on my left while I was making
calls. When I hung up the phone from talking to Marni, I
turned towards him. He wore black plants and a wrinkled
white shirt with some strategically placed food stains. He
needed a shave and his hair was disheveled. He looked to be
about fifty years old, with the eyes and complexion of someone friendly to alcohol. Was he a patient, a doctor, a minister?
I didn't know. Finally, he broke the silence.

"Mr. Levitt…"

"Yes…"

"I am the coroner."

"You are the what?"

"Coroner."

What the hell does he want, I thought.

"I will have to do an autopsy on your daughter."

An autopsy? My mind flashed to a scene of Stacey
stretched out on a cold steel table while this guy… It was too
horrible to think about.

"Why?" I asked.

"It is the procedure in these circumstances."

My brain was rapidly shutting down, but now I was faced with having to think of a way to avoid this. There was no way I was going to allow it. Knowing little about the legalities of such matters, I said, "There must be some way to avoid an autopsy."

"Give me a reason."

I was having trouble focusing, but I searched in my memory back to my criminal law course of some twenty-three years earlier. "She was hit by a car, there is nothing suspicious about that," I said.

The coroner looked at me blankly. Then a thought flickered in my mind. "We are Jewish and I object on religious grounds," I said.

"Okay, then, we won't do the autopsy," he said.

I was so relieved that for a split second I felt better. I had reduced the nightmares by one.

Until you have experienced amnesia, it is difficult to comprehend how completely some memories can disappear from your mind. The details from the time when I learned of Stacey's death through the time spent in the emergency ward of Sunnybrook are clear and vivid to me. But what happened next, how I got home, who was there, and what was said are gone. For several hours, I went missing from this world.

My recollections begin again with me at home on the telephone later that night calling people: my law partner, who was at the cottage next to mine at Thunder Beach; my brother, Frank, in Cooper City, Florida; and my closest friends. Such news is always horrific, but being woken up in the middle of the night accentuates the shock. My brother, roused from a deep sleep, heard my words being recorded on his answering machine and later said he was sure he was having a bad dream.

Not knowing what to do next, wanting to jump out of my own skin, I had to be in motion. I had to do *something*. The accident had occurred a short distance from our home, a mere seven-minute jog away, at the corner of Ledbury Street and Lawrence Avenue. I had few other facts. I began to walk north along the road Stacey must have jogged less than twelve hours before. What was I going to see? What could I accomplish? It really did not matter. I needed to be where she had been; where she had fallen; where she had left this world.

It must have been 2 a.m. by now. As I approached Lawrence from west of where the accident had occurred, I noticed a long piece of yellow police tape with the words POLICE LINE repeating along its length in big, bold, black letters. I touched it and stared at and tried to comprehend what had happened there only hours before.

It would be six weeks before I would know for sure what had happened and why. However, within days I would learn that Stacey, after coming home exhausted from her shopping and her shift as a lifeguard at the North Toronto Community Centre, had asked a friend, Amy, to go rollerblading with her. Being the athlete that she was, she was going to shake off her fatigue by exercising. Amy couldn't go, so Stacey decided to jog alone and was going to meet up with her later for dinner.

Stacey had been jogging on the spot, waiting for the light to change at the intersection. When she stepped off the curb, at 7:10, to continue running north, a car traveling east struck her and sent her somersaulting thirty feet in the air. She landed on her head. When the paramedics arrived she was "VSA," vital signs absent. They were able, however, to restart her heart and therefore took her to Sunnybrook

Hospital, where a trauma team worked on her until she was pronounced dead at 9:02 p.m. Had they not succeeded in getting a heartbeat, she would have been taken straight to the morgue.

She had no identification on her and the police began a frantic search for her family. Amy had been in a panic, because Stacey, a punctual person, was several hours late for their dinner engagement. She had gone to our house at around 8 and banged on the door, but no one was home. She returned to her house feeling that something was wrong. She turned on the television and saw a news report about the accident. There was no mention of the victim's name, of course, but Amy saw a picture of Stacey's running shoe on the road and called the police.

No insights, no answers, no relief. I wandered like a zombie back to my home.

When I arrived there, I could see that the house had filled with people. I do not know who they were and what they were saying, but I do remember feeling that it was good they were there.

Eventually our house emptied and Cheryl, Jacquie, and I were alone for the first time. We were exhausted, but sleep was impossible. Each of us needed to be silent now and alone with our own thoughts and feelings. Jacqueline retreated to her bedroom and Cheryl to ours. I spent the remaining hours of darkness in my home office trying to get in touch with reality.

CHAPTER TWO

goodbye

If loneliness and fear should seize you
in the black of night, fear not,
for love and hope
will come with the morning light.
UNTITLED POEM, STACEY LEVITT, 1989

MORNING ARRIVED AND SO DID A FEW OF OUR CLOSEST friends. It was time to go to the funeral home and "make arrangements" for Stacey. Unlike other religions that have a period before burial to view the deceased and grieve before interment, a Jew must bury the deceased almost immediately, out of respect for the deceased and because Jewish law prohibits embalming. There is no time to comprehend what has happened or what is happening. One minute you are embracing her, the next minute you are picking out a coffin.

And so, on Thursday morning, August 31, around 10, Cheryl, Jacqueline, and I found ourselves entering the office area of Benjamin's Funeral Home, one of the two funeral homes serving the Toronto Jewish community. Benjamin's used to be located downtown in the College and Spadina area, where Toronto's Jewish community had settled before and after World War II. With the subsequent migration of the Jewish community out of the city core, it was relocated to the north of the city, on Steeles Avenue near Dufferin Street. I had been to many funerals there, but never appreciated how much more there was to the operation. We were ushered into a room that was softly lit and warmly furnished.

Michael Benjamin took the meeting and gently guided us through all the decisions that had to be made. Where will Stacey be buried? How many limousines will be required? Should there be two police escorts or three? Everything seemed to move smoothly, as if we were in a routine business meeting. There was no trace of the horror that the meeting represented. I asked Michael to arrange for five plots, so our family could be together eventually.

Cheryl interjected that we needed only three. "Marni and Jacqueline will have their own families," she said.

How could she be so rational at a time like this? She was right.

"Ned and Cheryl," Michael said, "we now need to select a coffin. Please follow me."

We entered what is essentially a showroom for caskets. It was a very large room, made to feel even larger by the state of mind one possesses when entering it. Michael gave us a moment to collect our emotions and walked us around the room explaining the various choices.

"The law requires that I also show you a pine box, which is another option you have," he said.

We were standing there no more than eleven hours after I had identified Stacey's body in the hospital emergency room, selecting a coffin for that beautiful body, as if we were choosing some furniture for her room.

I learned later that Stacey's body lay all this time in a room close by. I did not realize that we could have seen her. I am sure I would have wanted to. I had not returned to the room off the hospital emergency ward to be with her and to hold her.

The casket chosen, the funeral arrangements discussed, we next went to the airport to await Marni's arrival from Montreal. Not much was said, but the fountain of emotion exploded when we saw her. She was escorted off the plane by a compassionate woman who had sat beside her and comforted her during the trip home. We then left the airport and headed home. My brother, now arrived from Florida, greeted me at the door. I collapsed in his arms. He would tell me later that my body felt like it was hollow.

Out of deep compassion for our family, Rabbi Dolgin came to our house late that afternoon to meet with us to prepare the eulogy, instead of our going to the synagogue, which is more customary. As he was asking each member of the family, one by one, about their experiences with and memories of Stacey, Cheryl slipped up to Stacey's room. She returned with a well-worn journal in her hand. It was Stacey's poetry journal, which she had kept since she was nine years old.

She handed the journal to the rabbi and said, "If you want to know Stacey, read this."

He took it reverently, as if it was an ancient and priceless artifact, and took his time turning pages and reading poems and parts of poems selectively. "May I take this with me?" he asked cautiously.

"Yes," Cheryl answered.

I did not sleep that night, save for momentary blackouts from exhaustion. Finally, it was 8:00 a.m., late enough to warrant preparing for Stacey's funeral. I stumbled into the shower and was astonished by the feeling of hot water on my skin. Each sensation was magnified several fold. The noise of the shower made me feel like I was standing under Niagara Falls. I looked at the drops of water on the shower walls with an intensity I had not experienced since I was a child. It was as if I had taken a mind-altering drug.

I felt I could not dress the way I would on any normal day. There was nothing usual about this day. I knew this day would be seared in my mind until I was laid beside her. I put on black socks, black suit pants, white shirt, dark tie, black shoes, black suit jacket. Then I reached for my watch. My watch? What relevance would time have for me today? For someone who measures a day in tenths of an hour, who fits in appointments like pieces of a jigsaw puzzle, who is always concerned about being on time and finishing on time, being without my watch would be like being naked. I placed it back in the jewelry case and went downstairs.

A long silver limousine was waiting outside the house. Cheryl, Marni, Jacqueline, and I, with bundles of tissues in our hands, swollen eyes, and hunched shoulders, slipped into the back of the limousine. We headed slowly towards Benjamin's.

When we arrived, we were taken into a room I knew about but had never seen: the family room. It was very spacious, richly decorated with calming colors and fabrics. One notable feature was the huge one-way tinted window installed on the wall separating the family room from the chapel. This allows the family of the deceased to view those in attendance without being seen themselves. With what was left of my rapidly deteriorating mind, I took note of several estranged couples who were finding their seats in the sanctuary hand in hand or with arms around each other. Benjamin's staff had to open the doors to combine all of the chapels in the funeral home to accommodate the thousand or more people who came, in disbelief and pain, to grieve with us and honor Stacey.

Rabbi Pearlson, the senior rabbi, who had been my rabbi since I was seven years old, took Cheryl's face in his hand, looked deeply into her eyes, and asked her, "Cheryl, if I could take away the excruciating pain that you feel right now, would you exchange it for never having given birth to Stacey?"

Cheryl sobbed and answered in a voice that was barely audible: "No."

Then he turned to me and said, "Ned, what you are about to do is for Stacey. It is the last thing you will do for her and it must be done."

The funeral director asked Cheryl and me if we would like to view Stacey. I would have preferred to have "seen" her, not "viewed" her, but I understood.

I went first. As I approached the casket, I saw her face. It was not the face of someone in easy repose. I could see anguish. Was it because of the trauma, or maybe because the last thing Stacey would ever want is to be separated from her family? The last time everyone else had seen Stacey, she was alive and vibrant. Not I. I had already seen her in this state. As I stood over her, for what reason I do not know, I turned to the funeral director, standing beside me, and asked, "Can I kiss her?"

What was I thinking? Why did I need permission from a stranger to kiss Stacey, alive or dead?

He answered simply, "Yes."

I was not prepared for the feeling of her cold forehead on my lips. It was like kissing marble.

Cheryl, Marni, and Jacqueline followed behind me for their last few moments with Stacey.

As for the service itself, it may have taken a half hour, or half a day, I really don't know. I had no watch on and no sense of time. I drifted in and out of reality and was not much aware of what was being said, only of who was saying things. I do remember that Stacey's four closest friends since pre-kindergarten, Lori, Tara, Joanne, and Rebecca, spoke of her strength and talent, but most of all about her concern for them and others and her wish that the "Fearsome Fivesome" would always stick together. I was aware that the two rabbis were reading some of her poetry, but it was not until I heard a tape of the ceremony, years later, that I realized how much of her own eulogy Stacey had written. One of the rabbis read her poem "Why?" Stacey had written it in September 1990.

Why?

Why?
Why is a question with no answer.
No one knows why.
Why is the sky blue?
Why is the grass green?
Why is there war?
Questions with no answers.

Not for a moment
is there not a question to be asked.
And it almost always starts
with the annoying little word,
why?
What frustration this insignificant
word can cause.
What problems come up
when someone utters those three letters.
Why?
Who knows why?
Not a single soul knows the answer.
So much confusion
and questions unanswered.
Why?

The four of us filed out of the funeral home past those who had come to mourn. The look on everyone's face reflected the tragedy of attending a funeral for such a young woman.

Our limousine was just behind the hearse. We were not aware of the length of the procession behind us as it snaked its way up to the Pardes Shalom cemetery, which is, at normal times, a good fifteen-minute car ride north of Benjamin's on Dufferin Street. We were told later that the procession was one of the longest ever seen for a funeral. The mourners turned slowly into the driveway and through the iron gates of the cemetery. As terrible a place as it is for those who must go there to bury their loved ones, it is beautiful, with rolling hills and mature trees in a rural setting.

We sat for a long time after arriving while everyone who was attending the interment parked their cars and positioned themselves for the procession to Stacey's gravesite.

As I stepped out of the limousine, I was numb. My numbness was briefly penetrated by the sight of her friends, in two lines, waiting to carry her coffin.

The sun was brilliant and it was hot. At the gravesite, I held my family close, very close, and turned my face up towards the sun with my eyes closed. The searing heat felt soothing on my face. Periodically, I lowered my head and opened my eyes and gazed on those assembled, trying to comprehend what was going on. Then I quickly returned to looking at the sun through closed eyes.

"Yit-gadal V'yit-kadash Sh'may Raba, B'alma D'hu Atid L'itchadta, Ul'achaya, Metaya, Ul'asaka L'chayey Alam, Ul' mivneh Karta D' iyerushalem, Ul' shachlel Heychala B' gava… May his great name grow exalted and sanctified in the world which will be renewed, and where He will resuscitate the dead and raise them up to eternal life, and rebuild the city of Jerusalem and complete His Temple with it…"

As the cantor chanted the ancient prayers and the coffin was lowered into the grave, I looked at my two remaining daughters and wondered how this was affecting them and what they were thinking at that moment. I glanced to my left and one row over, at a fresh grave. Its temporary marker read, "Heather Cloth, July 9, 1995." My cousin, at forty-two, had lost a courageous, two-year battle to the scourge of breast cancer. I looked at her husband, Marty, and her two young children, Casey and Alyssa. Tears were cascading down their cheeks. Seven weeks earlier we had been here grieving with them. Had Stacey stood then on the very spot where she was now being laid to rest?

The final act in burying Stacey was the covering of the coffin completely with earth. It is an honor and a duty for those assembled to take a shovelful of earth and throw it on the coffin. The funeral director turned to me and offered me, as Stacey's father, the highest honor of being the first to do so. The sound of the earth hitting her coffin, the thud, and then the hollow reverberation, sent shock waves through my chest. Had I not been in shock, I never would have been able to do it. Two weeks later, I could not have even lifted the shovel.

All that was required was that we cover the top of the coffin completely. Usually, the assembled mourners then leave the cemetery, and the grave is filled in by a machine. In fact, I could hear and see that another grave off in the distance was being filled in that way. But I was determined that Stacey's grave was not going to be filled in by a machine. I requested that we finish the job with shovels. Our family and friends worked purposefully and diligently, in spite of the extreme heat, and the crowd stayed together longer than is normal.

"Are we finished?" I asked several times. I did not really know what a completely filled in grave looked like.

When we were told that the job was done, I reached down to take a handful of soil to place the last of it on my daughter's grave with my bare hands. The soil was from the hole and its surprising softness and silkiness had a calming effect on me, knowing that this was what surrounded Stacey now.

During the burial, I was aware of a presence to my left and just behind me. I saw it was my father, looking unbelievably frail and sickly but standing resolutely during the proceedings. A thought flickered in my mind that I should try to comfort him, see if he was all right, maybe get someone to give him the opportunity to sit down. My father was seventy-six years old then and had many things wrong with his health. In his forties he had suffered a series of heart attacks, clearly contributed to by a sedentary life, poor eating habits, and addiction to tobacco.

My mind flashed back twenty-seven years, to 1968. My father was already in the hospital, recovering from another in a series of heart attacks, when he went into cardiac arrest and was rushed from his room to Intensive Care. He was clinically dead for several minutes, but they revived him. Prior to that, the only loss I had known was of grandparents and an aunt, which saddened me but did not have the impact of that moment. While we waited outside the ICU, for the first time in my life I tasted grief. My mind and body were already reacting to loss, sending adrenaline coursing through my body, drying my mouth, shortening my breath, and leaving me light-headed. My legs were weak. My mother's hysteria, everyone's confusion and alarm, all contributed to the feeling of dread that was washing over me. He was lucky that he was already in the hospital when the cardiac arrest occurred or he would never have lived.

As the mourners around me finished filling in the grave, I concluded, calmly, matter-of-factly, that he was going to die before the funeral was over or shortly after that. I had no strength and no will to help him. I turned back to the surreal scene unfolding before me.

Rabbi Pearlson asked those assembled to make a path for the mourners by forming two lines. Cheryl, Marni, Jacqueline, and I then turned away from Stacey's grave. Clutching each other, we began walking the path thus created. It was the only path available to us, and where it led we did not know. Suddenly, we heard a shriek from behind us. Everyone looked back towards the grave, where my sister, Lisee, had begun wailing. We continued on.

The four of us half fell into the back of the limousine. Jacqueline put her arms around Cheryl's waist and put her head on Cheryl's chest. Cheryl's arms gently enfolded Jacqueline's body. Marni laid her head in my lap and I stroked her hair. As the limousine maneuvered its way around the cemetery towards the iron gates and the exit, Marni's arms reached out towards Stacey's grave.

CHAPTER THREE

the journey begins

Set a goal
and reach it!
Hold your head high!
Don't settle for second,
be first!
Aim for the top,
use your power!
Let yourself go
up, up,
To the zenith of your being!
Believe in yourself!
You can do whatever you want
if you really set your heart to it!
"To Everyone," Stacey Levitt, 1989

MOURNING FOR A JEW BEGINS, LIKE SO MUCH ELSE IN JEWISH life, not in solitude, but amidst the hustle and bustle of the community. By the time we arrived back at our home, at about 1:30 p.m., the house was already teeming with people.

Virtually all of our female friends were engaged in arranging food on platters, brewing coffee, setting out utensils, and preparing for the onslaught yet to arrive. Food looms large in every aspect of Jewish life. One jokester summed up the Jewish holidays as, "...they tried to annihilate us, they failed, let's eat!"

By the end of the day, everyone had left, because it was Friday and the Sabbath was about to start, which meant that the beginning of Shiva, the seven days of mourning following the burial, would be suspended until after sundown on Saturday. During the first seven days following burial, Jewish law and tradition require that the mirrors in the house where Shiva will be observed be covered and that no music be played and no entertainment be conducted. The mourners are required to sit on chairs without cushions and on seats lower than those who come to comfort them. After sunrise and again before sunset, in the presence of at least ten Jewish males who have had their Bar Mitzvah, specific prayers are recited. Traditionally, friends or family of the mourners take over the responsibility of feeding the mourners and seeing to their needs. We had such people in abundance and a hundred or so men for each service.

As we waited for Shiva to begin, Cheryl and I were left floating in outer space. We had no idea what to do. We usually attended synagogue only on holidays or for weddings and funerals. But now it felt like we should go there. As we walked into the sanctuary at 8:00 p.m. that night, I felt completely out of place, even though I had attended services there all my life. I was completely detached from those in attendance, which seemed to suit them, since they felt uncomfortable seeing parents who had just hours before buried their daughter.

I tried to take part in the service. It was time for responsive reading:

> *Your deeds, O Lord, fill me with gladness,*
> *Your work moves me to song,*
> *How great are your works, O Lord!*
> *How profound Your design!*

The words stuck in my throat. I read of the eternal God, the God of mercy, the all-powerful God, and the God full of compassion and love for his flock, but I could not pray to a God who had taken away my Stacey — or, at least, had not protected her. But we just sat there, because, other than the cemetery, there was nowhere else Cheryl and I wanted to be.

The hot, sunny summer weather was continuing. By Saturday evening, our house was again filling quickly, and many people congregated on the front porch and the back deck. When you get a lot of people together like that, it is impossible to keep a festive atmosphere from evolving. This atmosphere, while so out of step with the horrible, tragic reason for the gathering, distracted me and helped me push back the demons that were gathering to feast on me.

As darkness began to settle on our home, a member of our congregation arrived to lead the evening prayers for a house of mourning. But the traditional prayers did not seem enough to me; they were not sufficient to capture who Stacey was and the pain all of us were feeling from losing her. I reached for her poetry journal, which Rabbi Dolgin had returned, and read two of her poems, "The String of Life" and "Why?" At every Shiva I have ever attended, the noisy, festive atmosphere resumes right away once evening prayers are over. Not this time. No one spoke for a very long time.

Then, amidst a quiet murmur, everyone slowly embraced those close to them and our family and left.

What passed for sleep ended at about 7 a.m. on Sunday morning. I went downstairs only to find one of our dear friends, Elaine, already fussing in the kitchen, getting food ready for us (as if we could eat) and the visitors who would be streaming through our house that day. She had put on a pot of coffee and was boiling water for tea.

"Good morning, Elaine. Who let you in?" I asked.

"The door was open, so I thought I would get an early start," she said. "How are you doing, Ned?"

I just shrugged and made a face that spoke volumes. Then, by tacit agreement, the conversation drifted to the mundane and the banal. Neither of us had yet learned the language of this strange new land. She offered me a breakfast. I politely declined.

My friend since law school and former law partner, Rick, showed up in the middle of the afternoon. His calm wisdom had always been a source of comfort to me and now was no exception. Everyone wanted to help us, but most could do little more than watch us suffer. Rick wanted to help very badly. When there was a lull in the afternoon, he suggested we take a walk around the neighborhood. It felt good to walk with him and talk. He asked again if there was anything he could do for me.

"Rick, I need to know what happened," I said. "You are the only one I can trust to find out the truth."

We discussed the sketchy details that were known at the time and conjectured about the cause of the accident. But conjecture was not enough for me. I wanted to know every detail of how Stacey died. Rick was a brilliant litigation lawyer, with a master's degree in criminal law from Berkeley and extensive experience in criminal cases and personal injury claims, including many car accidents.

"I am in no condition to find out for myself," I told him.

Rick agreed without a moment's hesitation, and I felt some relief. We continued our walk and decided to make it longer than we had planned. For the first time in a very long time during this summer of incredible sunshine, storm clouds were gathering.

"We might get caught in the rain, Ned," Rick said.

"I don't really give a damn. If it rains, I am just going to get wet," I said. At that very moment, we heard a loud crack of thunder. Within minutes it started to rain. I looked at Rick. He looked at me. "Let's run for it!" I shouted, and we raced down the sidewalk to my house laughing.

When we reached the house, I ran up the front stairs laughing and giggling with Rick, only to be confronted by the sight of a house full of distraught visitors who looked as sad as I must have looked happy. I did not know what to do. Apologize? Become somber quickly? Profess that I had lost my mind?

That evening, as the house filled to overflowing with people, Cheryl remained in our room, upstairs, too distraught to make small talk with well-wishers. As the time grew nearer for prayers, I went to our room to get her. As I walked in, I saw that Marni had joined her on the bed. I did likewise. Then Jacqueline came into the room and, without a word, also stretched out on the bed. With hands touching legs, legs resting against torsos, heads on stomachs, we must have resembled a scene from a Picasso painting. We lay there for a long time, not saying a word, simply needing to be close to each other. Until that moment, life had been draining from us. For the first time, it felt as if we were feeding life back into each other.

Then someone came into the room and said it was time to start the service. This time, I had prepared by selecting another two of Stacey's poems to read at the end of the service. I was pleased to see that reading her poetry had the same effect on these people as it had on the people the night before. A number of them wanted to get copies of the poems, including my lifelong friend, Brian, who had come with his wife to Toronto from their home in Weston, Florida, on hearing the horrible news.

"When are you going back to Florida?" I asked him.

"We are leaving Tuesday night."

"Would you help me make photocopies of Stacey's poems tomorrow morning?"

"Absolutely."

I wanted to have copies of Stacey's poetry journal out for people to see when they visited our home.

The next morning, Brian came by and we headed out to the business center with Stacey's poetry journal. It was strange to be out in the real world for the first time since I'd left it four days before. Nothing felt or looked the same. Streets and buildings I knew well, having lived in the neighborhood for the last twenty-one years, looked unfamiliar to me. I confessed to Brian that I thought I was losing my mind.

We entered the store, which was brightly lit and crammed with an incredible array of business machinery and computers. Most of the people there were students. I noticed that many were about Stacey's age, and I was hit by a wave of grief. I hid my eyes so they wouldn't see. It took me at least ten minutes to regain my composure.

Brian and I went about the business of obtaining coins and securing a photocopier for the task at hand. We had to be careful, in order not to damage the well-used journal, so we worked slowly.

"Can you imagine what the people here would think if I told them what we are doing?" I asked Brian.

"I don't think they would want to know," he said.

We returned to the house with ten copies of Stacey's poetry journal. We placed a few copies around our living room and stored the rest in my office upstairs. That night, Rabbi Pearlson paid a visit and I gave him one of the copies.

"Ned, this is very good," he said. "You should consider publishing it."

Publishing Stacey's poetry? When he mentioned it, I was reminded that publishing her poetry was one of Stacey's goals. In fact, in May 1988, she had won the prize for best poem in the Jewish Book Month Essay Contest, for her "When Does Shalom Come?" The Board of Jewish Education published the poem in its newsletter, to Stacey's great delight.

I wrote myself a note — I could not trust my memory right then — to look into to the possibility of publishing the poetry as soon as I was able.

The next morning, Tuesday, I sat at my kitchen table, with the newspaper laid out in front of me. I tried to read the lead article. I read a sentence or two, but it did not make sense. My mind wandered and I reread the same sentences over and over. They still made no sense. I tried another article; same result. Finally, I gave up in frustration and folded the paper and put it away. Maybe I would try a little later.

I got up from the table and walked to the front door, hoping the morning sunshine and fresh air would clear my head. I stepped out onto the front porch and into the bright sunlight. It was 8:30 a.m. and the sidewalks were full of students headed back to school after summer vacation. On the sidewalk directly in front of my house, headed west to the local public school, a steady stream of elementary school children, with colorful cartoon knapsacks on their backs, in groups as large as five or six, passed by. I looked across at the other sidewalk and saw a similar stream of high school students, with mountain gear knapsacks on their backs, walking east towards Northern Secondary School, Stacey's school. I began to shudder. I reached for a handful of tissue, which I now had to carry at all times in my pocket, and attempted to contain the tears welling up in my eyes.

As the pain began to subside, I noticed the letter carrier coming down the street. She was going from house to house, in typical fashion, but seemed to be struggling with her bag. As she reached our house, she came up to me where I was standing, on the front porch, instead of going to the side of the house, where the mailbox was.

"Good morning, Mr. Levitt," she said. "I have a lot of mail for you this morning." She struggled to hand me several armfuls of cards and letters. Then she said, "I am very sorry to hear about your daughter."

"Thank you," I said. I struggled back through the front door with the mail overflowing my arms.

I spread the mail out on the kitchen table and stared at it for a while. In front of me was a vast array of envelopes of varying sizes, colors, and shapes. Several hours passed before I had finished reading every letter and card, not just because of the volume of mail, but because of the time I needed to regain control over my emotions, as one heartfelt and beautiful note of condolence after another indicated grief that Stacey was gone and what an enormous loss this was, not only for me and my family, but for everyone who knew her and had been touched by her incredible, life-affirming warmth, sunshine, and generosity of spirit.

The volume of mail did not subside for weeks. This first batch was written by people who needed to react right away, to express their shock at such a sudden, tragic blow to our family. The very first letter I read stunned me. It was written by one of the most cynical, hard-bitten lawyers I knew. His message was, by contrast, touching and sensitive. Letters and cards that arrived weeks later were sent by those who could not initially cope with the heaviness of their sorrow and needed time before they could reach out to us. Each day, I would look forward to slowly and carefully reading each letter and card, even though I would invariably collapse in a sobbing heap when I finished.

Brian returned to Florida that night, and my brother the next day. Both departures left me feeling frightened and apprehensive, but there was no choice, they had to return to their jobs and families.

Shiva was to end on Friday, and we called to the synagogue confused and unsure about how it should end. Was there a service, a ceremony, prayers? We learned that though the seven days of mourning start with much ritual and ceremony, they end with nothing much more than a symbolic walk around the neighborhood. The director of the religious school connected to our synagogue was kind enough to come by and lead the walk and add some sense of finality to an unreal week.

"What do we do now?"

Cheryl posed the question, not really to me, even though I was the only one in the room at the time, but to the space around us, maybe to herself. I had no answers. The question was too big to even contemplate. What do we do now, without Stacey? What do we do now, with our family? What do we do now, with each other? What do we do now, with our lives?

It was best to start small, with the most immediate decisions that needed to be made. First, Marni was just starting her second year of university. Would she return to McGill? And when? The consensus on this issue was arrived at quickly and much more easily than the actual act of getting her ready and saying goodbye that Sunday night.

Not much was said as she packed her things and got ready to join the Alters for a car ride back to Montreal. Saul and Mirna were driving back to their city of origin to visit Mirna's ailing father. Saul took Marni's bags and put them in his car, while the three of us walked slowly, almost dirgelike, out our door, down the walk, and towards Saul's waiting car. At the car, we hugged and wept and tried to reassure each other that everything was going to be all right.

It was beyond frightening to see Marni disappear down the street in Saul's car. I wanted to run after her and stop her and keep her close to me so she would always be safe.

Re-entering our house after that required every ounce of strength we had. Jacqueline was reacting like most sixteen-year-olds. She was out of the house seeking comfort and support from her friends. She had the added burden of facing the friends, teachers, and hallways of Northern Secondary School that she had shared with Stacey.

The house was a dark, bleak, silent mausoleum now. The silence was broken only by the sobs emanating alternately from the two of us.

The Friday that Shiva ended, I needed to leave the house; I felt like I was suffocating. Personal hygiene had not been high on my agenda that week and, in the orthodox tradition of my faith, I had stopped shaving. Along with the rapid loss of weight and black circles under my eyes, the emerging beard made me appear every bit the suffering remnant of a human being that I was. I showered and decided to call my barber, to see if he could take me late that afternoon. It seemed to be a good idea. I would get a badly needed haircut, have the growing beard shaped, have some conversation, and be touched. Also, the barbershop was close to my office and would give me a trial run at going downtown. I had developed some paranoia and was uncertain whether I could drive downtown, let alone go to my office.

I called Dave, my longtime barber, and he asked me if 4:00 p.m. would work.

"Okay," I answered.

"Ned, you sound funny. What's up?"

I didn't know what to say to him. Should I wait to get there and then explain? I felt it would be better to tell him now; it would make the appointment go better.

"Dave, my daughter died." I said.

Silence.

"I look like a mess and I am a mess."

"Ned, I am so sorry!"

My office is situated in the tallest office building in downtown Toronto, the Scotia Plaza. The parking garage is deep within its bowels and, to the newcomer, the long spiral ramp from the street to the parking garage can be frightening. I had descended this path a hundred times without a thought, but now I felt a rush of anxiety as I spun deeper and deeper underground. As I emerged from the parking elevator and started the trek through the underground maze connecting all of the major buildings downtown, I found myself uncharacteristically fearing that I would encounter someone I knew. I was lucky; no familiar face crossed my path. But as I moved among the strangers who shared the maze, I was convinced they all knew what had happened and were just being polite in ignoring me.

When I walked into the barber shop, all conversation stopped. Obviously, Dave had told everyone there what had happened. Little did I know, but his father had died suddenly only a week earlier. He and I had lots to share, and the personal attention, warm towel on my face, and hum of the hairdryer all worked to calm me. When I finished, I hustled back to my car without any thought of taking the elevator up to my office. I knew I could not handle that.

I left the decision to return to the office until later in the weekend. Long before the sun rose Monday morning, I was wide awake. I was not rested, more bored from tossing and turning. The night before, I had decided that I would go in to work. Now it was time to shower and put on my suit. I hoped preparing for work and going to work would make me feel human again.

Monday mornings, along with Wednesday and Friday mornings, were my typical workout times. I was a member of a gym in the same building complex as my office, which made it easier, in a hectic life, to be faithful to an exercise regime. I knew I would have no strength or inclination to work out that morning, and was unsure if I would have the strength or inclination to return to work.

The early hour allowed me to arrive at my office suite before everyone else and avoid the reactions of others as I made my way to my office. I closed my door, turned on the lights, and looked around. I wanted to run away. Everything I looked at seemed out of place, everywhere I went seemed wrong. I put my head down on my desk and let the tears flow.

I heard activity outside of my office as others were starting the workday, so I straightened myself up and opened the door. The members of the firm had all been at the funeral and had attended Shiva, so they had already become accustomed to my appearance and condition. Each person made a point of talking to me. The concern in their voices and the expressions of support relaxed me and allowed me to get myself under control.

I returned to my office and began to slowly examine the mail and retrieve telephone messages. I separated everything into two piles, one for business and the other for grief, leaving the grief matters to be dealt with at home later. As I was slowly sifting through the business material, someone knocked on the door frame of my now open door.

"Ned, my name is John Warren." Our six-lawyer firm shared space with the two-hundred-plus law firm of Borden, Elliot, one of the largest in the country. John was one of their senior partners. I did not know the reason for his visit, but gestured him in.

He closed the door behind him and I invited him to sit on my couch. I took the seat opposite him.

"I know how you feel, Ned," John said.

The thought flashed through my mind to ask him to leave. No one could know how I felt at that moment, not him, not anyone.

"My son died in a car accident three years ago. Welcome to the club that no one wants to be a member of."

What followed was more than an hour-long discussion about loss, family, and survival. John told me about his night of horror when the car his teenage son was a passenger in was wrapped around a light pole at the side of the Bayview extension in north Toronto.

John also told me about the Bereaved Families of Ontario, an organization that he said might be able to help me and my family. I made a note to contact them.

The meeting ended with a warm hug, and I thanked him more sincerely than I had thanked anyone in a long time. The value of his visit was chiefly in the fact that three years after his trauma he was still alive and able to work. Exhausted, I lay down on the couch in my office and slept.

I woke up forty-five minutes later feeling worse than when I closed my eyes. I gathered up everything in the grief pile and headed out the door, down the hall to the elevator, down to the parking level, and then into my car. The minute I shut the car door I fell apart. Crippled by spasms of grief, I sat there until I could finally start the car and head for the garage exit. Once I was on Adelaide Street, I dialed my brother, Frank, on my cell phone. Thank goodness he answered. As I drove, I talked and sometimes wailed. He comforted me when he could wedge in a word or two, but all that mattered to me, at that moment, was that he was listening to me.

It was now 3:00 in the afternoon. The fantastic weather was continuing. I parked the car in our driveway and sat there another few minutes. I did not want to go into my house. Finally, I got up the courage and went in the front door. I found Cheryl in our bedroom crying. I went to talk to Jacqueline in her room, but my words sounded hollow, and she needed her space. I tried sitting in my office and called Marni in Montreal, but there was little we could find to say to each other.

The next day, I arrived at work a little after 9. The place was like a beehive, both in our small section of the floor and on the rest of the floor occupied by Borden, Elliot. On my way in, I passed a few people who blurted out a "Good morning" but avoided eye contact. A couple of others, thinking I did not see them, ducked into a side hall to avoid contact with me. I felt like a leper.

After settling into my office, I began to ponder these reactions. Acting more on instinct than intellect, I got up from my desk. I started down the hall on a route around the entire floor, containing some thirty-plus offices. I stopped briefly at any office that was occupied, which at that hour was most of them. I had developed a workplace friendship with some of the lawyers and staff and a nodding acquaintance with others. Some were still essentially strangers. It did not matter to me which category they fell into. In turn, I said, "Hello, I am back, and I want to thank everyone at your firm for the kindness shown to me during this terrible time."

Many of the people in the firm had sent kind messages, and the firm as a whole had made a generous donation to the Stacey Levitt Athletic and Educational Fund we had quickly established to receive donations for future good works in her memory.

Depending on the color the person turned and the level of discomfort their body language projected, I lingered for some additional chitchat about nothing more intense than the weather or how the Blue Jays were doing.

Then I came to Frazer's office. Frazer was the head of their technology law department. As I was completing my by now polished routine, he said, "Ned, please sit down for a minute." I was glad for the rest. Then he dropped a bomb.

"Ned, the man who was driving the car that struck your daughter is a friend of mine," he said.

I froze.

Frazer continued. "He lives in your general area and was on his way home from work. He is devastated and wants to meet with you and your family. He feels terrible."

My head was spinning. "I can't meet with him right now, Frazer. I don't even know for sure how the accident happened."

Frazer offered that the driver had not been speeding or drinking and that he had stopped to help in any way he could.

I was beginning to feel sick, so I thanked him and left his office, taking up the rest of my trip around the floor, which took the better part of the morning. When I was finally back in my office, I phoned Rick and told him what Frazer had told me. I asked him how the investigation was going.

"It's much too early for any hard conclusions," Rick said, "but it doesn't look like the driver was at fault."

The next day, my arrival at work and movement around the office was as relaxed and as close to normal as could be expected. This time no one avoided me.

Cheryl returned to her work as a medical librarian at a major hospital on University Avenue later that week, and I altered my travel schedule so I could drive her to her office each morning and pick her up each evening. Little was said in the car, either way.

At night, Cheryl needed seclusion and I needed company. The bereavement books — by then I was reading two at a time — were telling me that couples grieve alone and can be of little comfort to each other. Many nights, Cheryl would start to wail with such intensity that she seemed to be convulsing. I panicked, shadowing her around the house, trying to console her. I was really trying to stop her crying. I could not cope with the added burden of seeing her suffering. Even more, it shocked me to see in her the manifestation of the terrible pain I was feeling inside.

I turned to two of our closest friends, Joey and Ferne. Ferne I had known since public school and Joey since junior high school. We had been friends as couples from the time I met Cheryl, when I was seventeen. They are two of the most compassionate, kind people I have ever met. Our tragedy was hard for them, but they made themselves available to us any time, day or night. A pattern evolved: Cheryl would lose control, I would panic and call Joey and Ferne, and they would drop everything and come to our house to comfort her.

Of course, this pattern had to end. It was doing nobody any good.

One day, several weeks after Stacey's death, a letter arrived from a Marsha and Ben:

> Please accept our deepest sympathies.
> Although you don't know us, we know how
> you are feeling because we, too, lost our
> son, Joel, tragically seven years ago when
> he was eighteen years old. If there is any
> way in which we could be helpful to you in

the future, please call any time. Just know
that we are constantly thinking of all of you
and send our deepest support and prayers.

I called them immediately. Marsha answered the phone.
I thanked her for her kind letter.

"You are welcome," she said. Then, "How is it going,
Ned?"

"It's pretty rough, but I guess you know that."

"I do."

I proceeded to discuss with her at great length their
experiences, what details of Stacey's accident I knew, and
eventually about how Cheryl and I were reacting. When I
told her that I was frustrated trying to calm Cheryl down,
she lowered her voice and said, "Let her be. When she is
ready to stop crying, she will stop crying."

At the risk of violating a religious law (you are not permitted
back at the cemetery for thirty days after the burial), but not
really caring if we did, Cheryl and I had returned to the
cemetery the Sunday morning after Shiva ended.

As we drove through the gates on our own this time, I
noticed that there were a few people visiting their loved ones
in various sections of this vast cemetery. I saw some headstones with white cloths tied around them waiting for unveil-
ings and a couple of gravesites that had been dug and readied
for funerals later that day. Cheryl and I moved slowly and in
silence as we got out of the car and walked the same path that
we had walked the week before and along which Stacey's
friends had carried her coffin.

There is nothing uglier than a newly filled in gravesite, with its temporary metal and cardboard marker. This one announced, "Stacey Levitt — August 30, 1995." As we sat on the ground weeping, an acorn smashed to the ground, startling both of us. I looked around in a daze, trying to understand how the acorn had landed next to us when the oak tree was a couple of yards away. I was crying myself, but found it hard to stay there and watch Cheryl's torment. I went for a walk among the graves. I read various headstones and was surprised to see how many of them belonged to young people. I noticed a section of the cemetery in which someone had set up a small plastic table and chairs and some dolls as though for a child's play tea party. I was shocked to see this. I wondered about the pain the parents must have been in to have done this.

When I returned to Cheryl, she was standing and I embraced her and we cried in each other's arms. Neither of us wanted to leave. Finally, I made the first move and she followed.

As we drove back to the city from the cemetery, I broke the silence. "I suppose we might as well close up the cottage early this year," I said. Cheryl nodded her agreement.

With the High Holidays approaching, I arranged for Marni to fly home from Montreal. On her return to Toronto, she offered to help us at the cottage.

The next weekend the three of us headed north along Highway 400 towards Thunder Beach. I had cottaged at Thunder Beach with my family as a boy and then returned with Cheryl and the girls twelve years earlier. Thunder Beach meant a lot to me. It held many of the magical memories of my life and the lives of my girls. I enjoyed seeing the kids do the same things I had done as a boy and sharing the same experiences with them that my family had shared.

As you approach the end of Simcoe Road #6, you come to a hill that rests on top of the Nipissing Ridge. As you reach the crest of the hill, you see the most breathtaking and beautiful vision. As the hood of the car dips to descend the hill, you can see the turquoise water of Thunder Bay, the ring of white sand around its perimeter, the trees defining the east and west points of the bay, and the vast expanse of the cobalt blue waters of Georgian Bay beyond. Landmark islands — Giant Tomb, Beckwith, and Christian — are clearly in view.

Over the years, I had witnessed the same view through the wondering eyes of a young child, then through the jubilant eyes of a schoolboy craving the precious summer delights that waited, and then through the proud eyes of a father anticipating the joys his children would discover. This day, as I slowed the car and finally brought it to a stop, I saw the incredible view through pained eyes. The knowledge that Stacey would never see it again cut slowly and painfully through my heart. The three of us sat there for a long time sobbing.

We accomplished the tasks necessary to close the cottage like three robots. We barely said a word. We finished the job as quickly as possible. The work done, Cheryl, Marni, and I took one last walk across the beach towards the water. The sun was warm, and we sat on the beach holding each other.

At that time of year, the beach is largely deserted. However, out of the corner of my eye, I noticed a couple walking towards us. They were relatively new to the Beach. I was not in the mood for an uncomfortable encounter if they did not know what had happened, nor for the discomfort of feeling my pain was being ignored if they did know.

Instead of passing us by, as I thought they would do, they came right up to us, and one of them said, "We know how you feel!" There was that phrase again. "Our son resides in a hospital in Texas. It is the only place that can handle his condition since his car accident years ago. He received severe head injuries as a young man in a car accident and now has the brain function of a child. "

We were drawn up short by the story and their bluntness. My thoughts began to circle around the question of whether I would be in less pain if Stacey were alive but with little or no quality of life. I thanked them for their concern, and we watched as they walked away with their arms around each other, wiping the tears from their cheeks.

CHAPTER FOUR

wall of pain

To know yourself is to lose
someone else.
UNTITLED POEM, STACEY LEVITT, 1992

O N SEPTEMBER 24, 1995, A MERE TWENTY-THREE DAYS AFTER
Stacey's funeral, Cheryl, Marni, Jacqueline, and I sat
down for our first Rosh Hashanah dinner without her.

From a spiritual, family, and emotional perspective, the
New Year celebrations (Rosh Hashanah through to Yom
Kippur) are far and away the equivalent of Christmas for the
Jewish community. Families gather around holiday meals
and go off together to synagogue for High Holiday services.
It is a time of introspection, atonement, renewal, and
remembering. People often compare Chanukah with
Christmas, but Chanukah, which is a minor festival in the
Jewish calendar, just happens to fall within the very powerful
and compelling Christmas season.

The dinner table is such an important place and strong symbol in the life of a family. Around this table, family issues are discussed, family battles are fought, birthdays and anniversaries are celebrated, and love is exchanged. Mealtimes and dinner tables are just about the only time and place that active families, with their busy schedules, get to see each other. So when a member of the family dies, it is no small problem to decide what to do about the seat that person occupied at the table. Some families deliberately switch seats to avoid staring at the one, now empty, that was occupied by the deceased. However, to solve the problem, one member of the family has to be courageous enough to assume the empty seat as their own.

That day, Cheryl was at home preparing the holiday meal while I was at the office struggling to accomplish anything that even remotely resembled productive work. My thoughts kept returning to my image of what that evening would bring. I was preoccupied by a problem I never dreamed I would have to face. Should I ask Cheryl to set a place for Stacey at the table? I did not believe I could endure the evening if it were not there. Having a place set for her would be a gesture that would transcend symbolism. It would be a statement that she was not gone completely from our lives. But how could I ask Cheryl to do this? Would it hurt her more? Finally, I concluded that I would not inflict my needs on her.

I walked into the house with a heaviness in my chest and a feeling of foreboding. My heart skipped a beat when I looked into the dining room and saw that Cheryl had set Stacey's usual place at the table. I felt a mixed emotion of joy and sadness. Perhaps the bereaved could coin a new word, "sadjoy," to describe such emotions. Marni had flown in from Montreal to be with the family for this very special and difficult night.

We eat in the dining room only on special occasions. Our home is very old and has lots of wood trim and leaded glass. The dining room is transformed on such nights by Cheryl's exquisite taste for antiques and becomes a scene that one of the great masters might have painted. Each plate and serving utensil has a story and a character all its own. On this night, as on so many before, the table was set with the holiday candles, the Kiddush cup for the wine, fresh apples, a dish of honey, and challah bread. Challah is a sweet and spongy egg bread. As I looked at it, I could see Stacey burying her face in a thick slice so that she could better inhale its delicious aroma.

Cheryl began the service by reciting the prayer for candle lighting and lighting the two holiday candles: "May Thy light, O God, enter our home at the beginning of this New Year and remain with us. May it be Thy will to grant us health and peace, prosperity and fulfillment." Those words fell hollow on my ears. What could God possibly give us to replace what we had lost?

It was my turn next to bless the wine: "May our cup of life be filled with blessing." The words and the wine tasted bitter to me.

Jacquie was next to say the blessing while we dipped pieces of apple into the honey: "May it be God's will to grant us a good and sweet year." What an ironic prayer for a family now faced with a year of intense pain and suffering.

Before the meal, at the end of the service, as hundreds of thousands of fathers were doing at that very moment, I walked around the table and put my hand on Marni's and Jacquie's head in turn to say a silent blessing for that child and the year ahead. I prayed first for Jacquie, and then for

Marni, but when I came to Stacey's empty place, I stood and cried until there were no more tears. I wasn't the only one crying. Finally, about twenty minutes later, exhausted, we settled down and finished our meal.

Marni, a talented writer and musician, wrote a song, "Too Early," about that first holiday dinner without Stacey, part of which reads:

> From the moment we sat down
> To our dinner marking the New Year
> We wondered how we could ever pass
>   through
> From the moment we unfolded the napkins
> And laid them on our laps
> We never thought we'd be doing this with-
>   out you
>
> *And we all get up from the table*
> *When we know it's time to leave*
> *But when someone leaves too early*
> *It's a really sad thing*
>
> From the moment we prayed to God
> That we weren't really eating without you
> We bowed as our father blessed anyway
> From the moment our eyes set on
> The flicker of the candles
> We could barely see them through the
>   streaming of our tears

From the moment we wondered
How we could ever sit around here
    together again
We took our first step without you
But it wasn't really without you, no it isn't
    really without you
But we're crying in our sleep just to hold
    you again
And when this stormy weather's passed
    through this year and this table
We'll be thinking of you, we'll be thinking
    of you

Each workday, during the first few months after the accident, it felt better to me to put on my suit and go to the office rather than stay at home. I did this even in the face of the cold hard truth that I was getting little done at work. A long list of good friends would call me, each day, for lunch and conversation. My partner in the law firm, Jeff, made it his practice to be available for lunch with me if I had run out of friends and needed to talk. Everyone grieves differently. My way was to go over and over the night of the accident, the facts known thus far about it, my thoughts and feelings, and how the family was reacting.

One friend described me later as "a giant vortex, sucking in strength and energy from one friend after another." As I would exhaust one, I would move on to another and continue to seek some relief from the constant pain. I found out later that an informal network of my friends developed a warning system for grief preparedness when I was on the prowl for the next victim. I was wrapped up in my own little world of confusion and hurt and not aware of how I was affecting others.

In one of the books I was reading, the author, a bereaved mother, asserted, with only a little exaggeration, that she could empty a grocery store in her small town simply by walking into it. By now, I was well aware that this extraordinary power had been bestowed on me.

As I was returning to my office building from another long, heart-wrenching lunch with a friend, I spotted the woman who had taught a course in conversational French that I had taken more than ten years earlier. She was walking towards me, just close enough for each of us to recognize the other, but just far enough for a discreet glance away so that an encounter could be avoided. Her face revealed a flicker of fear before she glanced away, and I wondered if she knew. Any doubt was erased when she deliberately and without any apparent reason crossed the street.

I determined in a flash that this was not going to be how I would live the rest of my life. I love contact with friends and colleagues and hate isolation. I crossed the street and headed towards her. Body language speaks louder than words sometimes. I could see her stiffen as if bracing for a hit.

"Bonjour, Catherine, ça va bien?"

"Ça va! Et toi, Ned?"

"Not so good."

"Yes, Ned, I heard about your daughter. I am so sorry!"

This was a warm but windy day with cars, taxis, and buses plying Bay Street. We fell into an easy conversation in spite of the bustle of the lunchtime crowd of Bay Street brokers, executives, professionals, and secretaries. Gradually her fear melted, as did my frustration with my newfound status as pariah. As we took leave of each other and I entered my building and got in the elevator to go up to my office, I realized that before Stacey's death I was no different from her, avoiding contact with those who carried the contagion of death.

Six weeks after the accident, my phone rang. It was Rick.

"I have completed my investigation of Stacey's accident and met with the insurance adjuster," he told me. "Ned, there is no doubt that the driver was not at fault."

I paused to let this news sink in. "I was expecting that, Rick. In a way, this takes an enormous burden off of me. I can't imagine how I would deal with the anger I would feel if he had done something wrong."

Rick went on in a tone mixed with professionalism and empathy. "As I think you know, even if the driver were at fault, the damages in the case of a child's death are very small."

"Yeah, I remember that from my law school days."

Rick continued. "However, the insurance adjuster has become very caught up in Stacey's story. As she interviewed people, she kept hearing about what an amazing person Stacey was. In fact, she kept working on the case from an interest point of view."

In a strange way, this gave me some satisfaction.

"In any event, she is willing to recommend to the insurance company that they make a significant payment to Stacey's fund."

By then, many friends and family had been generous with their donations and, along with Stacey's savings, payment from the firm's group life insurance policy, and a contribution from our family, her fund had grown to a significant amount. A payment from the accident would take the fund to a level that would allow us to salvage something positive from our tragedy.

"Thank you, Rick, for all your help. I'm glad I don't have to focus on the cause of the accident anymore. It was very consuming."

"Ned."

"Yes, Rick?"

"There is one more thing. The driver desperately wants to meet with you and the family."

"Yeah, Rick, I heard the same thing from one of the lawyers here at Borden, Elliot."

"What do you want to do, Ned?"

"Let me think about it."

For the remainder of the day and deep into that night, that is almost all I thought about. I wondered was he old or young; was he a good person or bad; what could we possibly say to each other? Even if he was innocent of any wrongdoing, he was still the person who drove the car into Stacey and killed her. In some ways, the driver was the last person I wanted to meet. At the same time, I felt drawn to him. After all, he was there, his life and what remained of Stacey's crossed at that moment in time in a way that would forever change my life.

I canvassed Cheryl and the girls. Cheryl left little to doubt. "Ned, you do what you want. I want nothing to do with him." Marni was more ambivalent, but finally decided she just could not handle the emotion of such a meeting. When I asked Jacqueline, she just looked at me as if I had grown antlers.

I didn't want this encounter, either, but it felt like something that needed to be done. The next day, I phoned Rick and asked him to set the meeting up.

Rick made the appointment for first thing Wednesday morning, October 18, at his office, which was not far from mine.

"Ned, I have written a complete report on the accident. Why don't you and I have breakfast before the meeting? I can give you the report then."

We arranged to meet at 8:00 at a restaurant across from his building. I hung up the phone and felt a wave of anxiety wash over me. I had no idea what this meeting would be like or what it would accomplish. There was nothing in my experience on which I could draw to help me envisage what would transpire. By then, all I knew was the meeting was going to take place and I could not resist the force that was moving me towards it.

I arrived at the restaurant before Rick and took a table that allowed me to watch the front door. The restaurant was starting to fill up with the Bay Street crowd, but I remained oblivious to them. When Rick arrived, I was already full of apprehension. Quick pleasantries were exchanged, and I reached for the envelope he had removed from his briefcase and put on the table beside him.

"We better order some food, Ned."

Rick approached everything in life with passion, including, and maybe especially, food.

I answered in the affirmative, but I was not hungry. All I could do was stare at the envelope. Rick ordered a breakfast a lumberjack would be proud of, and I ordered a bagel and tea.

I turned the envelope around several times in my hands, not rushing to open it. I knew that Rick's work would be thorough, that he had done what I had asked him to do — that the truth about how Stacey died would be in that envelope. He had not sealed it, so all I had to do was lift the flap and slide the contents out. There was a covering letter from Rick, a memorandum to his file, a police accident report, the driver's statement to the police, and the statements to the police given by several eyewitnesses. I read in the letter the words: "…the accident was unavoidable. There was nothing that the third-party driver could have done to avoid hitting Stacey."

I read on. "For whatever reason, Stacey simply left the curb. The third-party vehicle was traveling at approximately the speed limit. Evidently, Stacey was standing between two poles when she left the curb. A combination of the poles, Stacey's own inattentiveness, or the setting sun in the west might explain why she did not see the car approaching. It was also apparent that she had her Sony Walkman headset on, which, presumably, would have impeded her ability to hear the oncoming traffic."

I felt my throat tightening up.

"Immediately upon impact, Stacey was thrown some substantial distance in the air. Apparently she did a number of somersaults before landing squarely on her head. She was unconscious at the scene and never regained consciousness."

As I began reading this last sentence, my legs started to shake uncontrollably and tremors spread throughout my body until I was twitching like someone having a seizure. Then I struggled to make out the words because I could not clear the tears from my eyes.

Rick asked, gently, "Maybe we should put off the meeting to another time?"

I slowly regained my composure. "No, Rick, I still want to go ahead with it."

I continued to read the letter. "From a medical point of view, there is nothing that could have been done differently. Stacey was fatally injured at the scene and died without hope of recovery…"

When I had finished the letter, Rick and I sat without talking. Finally, I said, "So that's it. There is no one to blame."

"That's right, Ned."

I could put out of my mind any thoughts of suing the driver, as well as any doubts about the medical care Stacey had received. Rick knew what he had to do and had done it well. I was ready to meet the driver.

Rick escorted me into a small meeting room. The insurance adjuster, a woman, having been caught up in Stacey and her story through her investigation of the accident, had wanted to be at the meeting. She was in her mid to late forties and was wearing a bright summer dress, reflecting the continuation of the summerlike weather throughout that fall. She remained in her seat as I entered the room. She had a warm smile for me, but when our eyes met, I saw a flicker of apprehension.

The only other person in the room was the driver. He stood as I entered the room and I looked at his face. He had a dark complexion, with features that subtly revealed his Southeast Asian roots. We were about the same height, five feet eight inches, so our eyes met directly. I saw no fear, no uncertainty, no nervousness, just pain and need. I felt numb. I already knew he was an engineer, drove a dark green BMW, and had a responsible position with a large corporation. Frankly, the details of his life were unimportant to me. I stood frozen in place until Rick pointed to one of the empty chairs across from the door.

The meeting table was round and of modest size, so there were no chairs that implied any stature or predominance.

Intimacy was assured. There was no agenda. I had no idea what I would say, and apparently neither did he. We all just sat in silence for a few minutes.

I was the first to speak. "I know you have wanted to meet with my family, but my wife and other daughters just cannot do that right now."

The driver nodded his understanding.

I went on. "My friend, Rick, has thoroughly investigated the accident and satisfied me that you were not at fault. I have heard and would understand that this has been a very difficult time for you. I want you to know that no one in our family blames you. If it helps, I forgive you."

The man's body almost deflated, and his eyes welled up with tears. "I am so sorry for what has happened," he said. "Is there any way I can help you and your family?"

I thought about this request for some time before responding. "Please tell me what happened." I listened to his version of the accident. Except for one small but important matter, he added nothing I did not already know.

When he came to the part about the impact, he hesitated and asked me if I wanted to know everything.

"Everything," I said with emphasis.

He said that when the car struck Stacey he could see her face and expression clearly. "It was as though she was saying, 'Where the hell did you come from?'"

Amazing. This was vintage Stacey. That is exactly what she would have said. For this reason, the fact did not shock or disturb me, at least not at that moment. I was, however, a little surprised that he would have chosen those words. When he finished telling me all that he knew, he renewed his request to help the family in some way. He had heard that we had set up a fund and wanted to make a donation to it.

He was a good person. I knew that he had stayed at the accident scene and tried to help in any way he could. I also knew that he was suffering terribly, just as I would have been, if I were in his place. There were two sets of shoes I did not want to walk in at that moment.

I replied, "In Hebrew, the word for life is *Chai. Chai* also is the word for the number eighteen. As a result, financial gifts are often given totaling eighteen or some multiple of it. Stacey made it to eighteen, and I choose to believe she therefore made a life. For whatever comfort that brings." I did not know his financial circumstances, and I did not want him, in his time of extreme emotional stress, to make an enormous donation that might hurt him financially. "I would ask you then to donate $18, no more and no less, to Stacey's fund," I said.

He nodded his agreement.

"I don't want to ever see you again. Not because of any negative feelings towards you, but because of the circumstances that brought us together. However, because we live in the same general area and there are some connections, I may hear about how you are doing in the future. It would not help me or my family if, in time, we learned that you were still suffering. Please help yourself and get this behind you. There are too many victims of this terrible accident already. One less would be a blessing."

The meeting ended in our embrace. Everyone in the room was in tears. I left with a feeling of some relief.

The impact of that meeting was brought home to me when Rick, moved by what had happened, had the kindness to send a letter to me:

> I wanted to drop you a note to tell you how
> remarkable our meeting last Wednesday
> was. From a professional perspective, in my

almost 20 years of practicing law cases of this nature, I have never seen such a display of grace and sensitivity as I did with you at the meeting.

It was evident to me that Stacey was sitting beside us and helping us all. As in everything else in her life, those who touched her and were touched by her were all the better for it. A seasoned and hard-nosed insurance adjuster was reduced to tears by the feelings in the room. Stacey would have been proud of all of us.

I am proud to be your friend.

The unseasonably warm weather lasted throughout October that year. However, on November 1, winter arrived, as suddenly and violently as any I could remember, in the form of a major snowstorm. The cold weather did not leave until well into May the next year. The beginning of November also marked the beginning of my third month of what I thought was grieving for Stacey. What I did not know was that I had been dealing, to that time, with trauma, not grief. Trauma, as anyone knows who has taken a hit in sports or been in an accident, has the capacity to numb or anesthetize you for a while from the pain. However, unlike the damage done to you when you are physically injured, this type of emotional injury occurs over a very long time after the blow is received. Some would explain that shock allowed me to do what I had to do in those first couple of months and protected me from being overwhelmed and destroyed by the devastating pain. I prefer the explanation that I was still functioning with most of my brain intact, as the reality of Stacey's death was slowly gnawing through it. The worst, by far, was yet to come.

As I descended into the depths of true grief, I could not believe how much worse was the pain I was now feeling. Unlike physical wounds, which usually heal in an upward trajectory, the wound from profound loss tends to worsen for a long time before healing starts to take hold very, very slowly. Anxiety and depression are the footmen to grief, and the downward spiral adds an element of fear that you are headed in the wrong direction, never to surface a whole person again.

My virtually daily phone calls to my brother began to intensify. Sometimes I called him four or five times a day. No matter what he was doing, he stopped to take my call and stayed on the line as long as I needed him. He, more than anyone else, could judge my condition, listen when needed, and speak to me in ways that, however fleetingly, helped.

"Oh God, Frank, I can't take it. I want to scratch out my eyes. What am I going to do, what am I going to do? I can't go on without Stacey."

"Ned, she wants you to get through this."

"I know, but I… I can't, I just can't."

"Ned, if you had died, what would you want Stacey to do?"

This stunned me. "What would I want her to do? I know what I wouldn't want her to do, that's for sure. I wouldn't want her to waste her life grieving for me."

"That's right, Ned, but you would also expect that her love for you could not be severed so easily."

"Yes."

"In a way, Ned, your enormous pain is the cost of loving her as much as you did and do."

"The cost of loving her?" That made me think. In fact, being brought up short like this, forced to think, momentarily halted my slide into the black hole of despair.

I raged and raged. I bargained with God to take me and bring Stacey back. I cursed him. I pleaded with him. I begged him.

I traveled through the darkest tunnels of my psyche. I visited the cemetery and tried to look through the soil to see her. Then I tried to block out the images that exploded in my mind of what was happening underground. I struggled to find the words to tell my friends and brother what all this felt like. I would say, "Imagine you are hanging over the edge of a very high cliff, grasping a thin branch as your only anchor, with certain death below you. Now imagine how you would feel at the moment the branch broke and you started to fall. Then try to imagine that feeling lasting for weeks."

As the weeks became months and there was no relief, I started to believe that the only solution was to join her. I began to think of a plan.

CHAPTER FIVE

i am a rose

I am a rose.
I drink the purest of
waters.
I stand big and tall
in my brand new vase
and when people walk by
they stop and gaze
at my wonderful, yet delicate,
petals of red.
Then they totter off swinging
their heads.
And with a backwards glance,
they run down the aisle
in a skip or a prance!
"I Am a Rose," Stacey Levitt, 1986

I HAD NEVER BEEN A VICTIM OF DEPRESSION OR ANXIETY. In fact, from birth, I was seen as someone who was very resilient, always happy, and incurably optimistic. Not anymore. The early stages of profound grief are almost indistinguishable from depression and are often accompanied by severe anxiety. In the first few months after Stacey's death, I frequently spent hours curled up on the daybed in my home office, in a blanket I folded around me like a cocoon, afraid that I would become the victim of a home invasion crime. I feared for my family's safety. I worried that I could no longer work and we would go broke. I felt bone-rattling fear, without knowing what I was afraid of.

There was one thing I was not afraid of during that period: dying. In fact, I wanted to die. The method that was the most appealing to me was to step in front of a car. This not only would end my anguish, it also would allow me to feel what Stacey felt.

Being an incorrigible planner, I wanted to explore every aspect of such a move. Where would I do it? At the same place Stacey left this world seemed logical. When would I do it? At night. What would I wear? Anything, as long as it was clean. What should I put in my note? I would have to explain to Cheryl, Marni, and Jacqueline that I could no longer stand the pain. I would ask them to understand and forgive me for leaving them to survive on their own.

But then I would picture them returning to Benjamin's for my funeral. I saw their faces as they stood at the cemetery and watched me being buried next to Stacey. How could I do that to them? I struggled with my need to escape against my need to help my family through this terrible time. During that time I began to feel as though Stacey was watching me. My conflict only intensified as I began to think that she would be so terribly hurt if I abandoned everyone else. I wanted her to be proud of me.

As I began to move away from thoughts of suicide, I became even more fearful. How do you survive this? Though I was consuming book after book about the loss of children, there appeared to be no roadmap to surviving your child's death. Lots of inspiration and expressions of hope, but nothing concrete about what to do.

Among Stacey's many pursuits had been tae kwon do. I was so proud of her as she dove into that sport with the same energy and enthusiasm she brought to her many other sports. It reminded me of my own years spent in martial arts. At one of the tournaments Stacey won, I turned to Cheryl and with the glee of an obnoxious hockey dad said, "Did you see Stacey clobber that girl?"

Martial arts were appealing to me when I was young because they involved spiritual, mental, and emotional elements, as well as the physical ones. I remember my *sensei* saying to me, "Ned, you are always a student in life. One day you will be a student father, later you will be a student grandfather." If I was not going to kill myself, I had to figure out how to survive and heal. I was now a student bereaved father.

The first and easiest aspect for me to work on was the physical. I had always believed in the importance of mind/body balance and knew that the body was where to start. I had lost a lot of weight, for me — some ten pounds — and my physical strength had dwindled. I was also experiencing extreme bowel cramps. Someone explained to me later that grief usually settles in one part of a person's body. The part depends on the individual. I had also read that intense emotional trauma can attack the immune system, with the incidents of disease going up dramatically for bereaved parents. I made a trip to the doctor, who agreed that he should monitor me more closely for at least the first year.

Being open to new ideas as never before, I took a friend's advice and went to a practitioner of Eastern medicine for help with the cramps. After I told him why I was there, he proceeded to treat me with acupuncture for my immune system and then for the cramps. I chose not to take any medication, opting, instead, to drug myself naturally with exercise. I resumed, as best I could, my workout routine. I did, however, add one more physical activity. I had never been much of a runner. When I had run in the past, everything seemed to hurt afterwards. This time, I purchased the right kind of shoes and started jogging several times a week.

One Sunday in late November, at about 10 in the morning, I warmed up at home with some situps, pushups, and stretches. I laced up my running shoes and exited the house. Despite the cold weather, I felt energetic. Instead of running my usual route west along Briar Hill Avenue and along the abandoned railway line, known as the Belt Line, I found myself turning east. After a few strides, I turned north along Mona Drive. I realized what I was doing. I was trying to trace Stacey's route to where the accident occurred.

All I knew was when it occurred, what direction she was headed, and the time she was to meet her friend Amy for dinner. From those facts, I was pretty sure I knew the route she had taken until she was hit and where she would have been heading (oh how I wish it were so) had she lived.

It felt good to move my body. I filled my lungs with air. It helped to clear my head. I started to get into the rhythm of the run along the fairly long stretch up Mona. Then I pictured Stacey running along the same road and checking her watch, because she would not have had a lot of time to finish her run, shower, and meet Amy.

I looked around at the houses as they slowly moved in and out of my frame of vision, listened to the wind in my ears, glanced at the blue sky with only a few puffy clouds in it, and wondered if this was what Stacey saw.

I reached Coldstream Avenue and turned west. My chest was now heaving, both from the heavy breathing from running and because I was crying. A few hundred yards later, I turned north onto Chicoutimi Avenue. As I approached Lawrence Avenue, I found it difficult to breathe from the strain of the two activities. At Lawrence, I turned right and headed the short distance east to where it intersects Ledbury Street.

When I reached the corner, I stopped and stared at the place where the police report said she had landed. I tried to imagine what happened there that night, but the thoughts began to sap me of energy, and I wanted so much to finish the run. As I began to run north from the intersection of Lawrence and Ledbury, my breathing settled down. I was filled with the feeling that I was finishing Stacey's run.

This became my regular run.

Strengthening my body was relatively easy compared with what it took to shore up my dwindling mind, emotions, and spirit. I was directed by Emily at Bereaved Families of Ontario to a bereaved mother and nurse named Susan. I read her article about the death of her teenage daughter, Kristina. Susan was eager to help me. I was learning quickly about the deep, mysterious connection and compassion that exists in the bereaved community. Susan told me about bereavement sites on the Internet. The thought of looking to the Internet as a source of support had never crossed my mind. Particularly, she alerted me to a newsgroup, alt.support.grief (ASG). This bulletin board site invites you to post a message to everyone and then allows others to comment on what you posted if they wish to. Bill Chadwick is the gentleman who put it together and keeps an eye on things and frequently is there to help people, particularly the newly bereaved. He helped me.

An advantage of the program is that you can log on late at night when you can't sleep and see that others are going through the same difficult process and find out how they are coping.

Bereaved Families of Ontario was started by five bereaved mothers. Its initial focus was to support newly bereaved parents, but it expanded to help children who lose parents, and siblings and grandparents of deceased children. At the heart of their support activities are the twelve-week bereavement groups led by bereaved parents who have completed a twelve-week session and gone on to be trained as facilitators of future groups. It was a very comfortable and natural path for me to take. The help I gave to other parents came back to help me just as much.

I began to share Stacey's poems with the people I encountered at and through BFO. Everyone loved them, reacted emotionally to them, and wanted copies for themselves, family, or friends. Some people told me that one poem or another helped them, or someone they knew, with their pain. A bereaved father I met through the Internet directed me to a website, webhealing.com, where I found a lot of information about loss and healing. You are invited to post, on the "Honor Site" of this website, a memorial to your loved one. I found reading the various postings made me feel less alone. I resolved then and there to post a memorial to Stacey. This is what I wrote, and it has remained on the site to this day for anyone to read.

On August 30, 1995, our daughter
Stacey was taken from us suddenly and
tragically in a traffic accident. She was
struck by a car while she was jogging. She

was 18 years old, a superior athlete, a top student and loved by so many. She was beautiful and had a special gift of relating to people in a way that enriched them and her. She didn't just live life, she devoured it. There didn't seem to be enough time in the day to do all of what she wanted to accomplish, but what she did accomplish in her brief life amazes everyone. She had set her sights on a career in medicine and would have entered university next year. We who knew her well have little doubt that she would have succeeded.

All of this sounds like a movie script which was written to evoke sadness and despair. As her father, I wish to God that it was a movie script. But in all of our grief we have come to realize that there is a message in how Stacey lived her life and how we were as a family, which may be of some comfort and inspiration to other parents and teenagers. We are able to find the strength to carry on, because our hearts are devoid of regrets or anger. We could not have spent any more time with Stacey, hugged her, kissed her, or told her we loved her more than we did. These were daily occurrences. She gave us back double of what we gave to her.

By striving to be the best that she could be, by willingly receiving love and giving love unconditionally in return, Stacey filled her life with joy and meaning and left us with a storehouse of wonderful memories. Her greatest legacy to us is her poetry, which she began writing at an early age. Her poems show a sensitivity and wisdom well beyond her years and serve to comfort us in our time of sorrow. We intend to publish her writings, so others can enjoy them and benefit from her insight.

She was my dive buddy, my tennis partner, my rollerblade pal, my soul mate, my best friend. I have been told that the amount of pain I feel is the measure of the love I have for Stacey. If this is true, I love her more than any words could possibly describe. Thank you for listening to my story.

— HER FATHER, NED

I included in my posting two of Stacey's poems, "Encounter with Death" and "I Am a Rose." I took the option to include my e-mail address for those who might wish to correspond with me. What amazing things happened as a result! I began to receive e-mails from people from all over who happened by the site and were touched by what I had written. Many of them wrote about Stacey's poems. For example:

I just read your daughter's poems. I don't know how I'm even typing because I'm crying...

Thank you for posting Stacey's poems and your story on the web. It was a great comfort

to me. It's a true gift when someone who has
already passed on can still touch a perfect
stranger here on earth. It's clear to me that
she lives on…in you and her poetry.

From the moment that Rabbi Pearlson had suggested we
publish Stacey's poetry, it was constantly on my mind. I
decided that we would do it. From conception to publication,
it would take nine months.

Only weeks after Stacey's funeral, I was looking for a place
to start the publishing project, but my inability to concentrate
and the emotional battles I was waging slowed the project
down. One Saturday morning, I opened the paper and read a
long piece on Rosemary Sullivan, an accomplished poet, bio-
grapher, and professor of English at the University of Toronto.
Within days, she had a photocopy of Stacey's poetry journal
in her hands and a request from me for advice on how to
publish it. Rosemary wrote to me on October 11, 1995.

I have read your daughter's manuscript and
I find it very poignant. The poems are moving: they are clearly the work of a talented
young girl and exciting in their potential.
Had she lived, I am sure your daughter
would have become an interesting writer
of whatever kind. Her vision is precocious;
she had an unexpected sophistication in
the way she saw the world as a child.

However, I think, given the current
economics of publishing, when so few books

of poetry are being accepted anyway, it would take a long time to find a publisher. My advice would be to publish the book yourself. It could be made very beautiful and would be a moving tribute to your daughter's talent and to her memory.

The best publisher/printer I can think of who does beautiful books is called Porcupine's Quill, run by a man called Tim Inkster. I phoned the press and was told they would charge around $2,000 for a fifty-page book, 500 copies. They will also input the text for you and do some general editing for an extra fee. However, your daughter's manuscript is so clean, and she obviously had such respect for her poems that she printed them carefully. There shouldn't be a lot of editorial work to do.

I wish you the best of luck. I think your daughter would be pleased if you did her book.

Shortly after that I called Tim, sent him a copy of Stacey's poetry journal, and made arrangements to visit his shop in Erin. Before driving to Erin, about forty-five miles northwest of Toronto, Cheryl and I stopped at the cemetery to visit Stacey. This visit to her gravesite took on a greater dimension. I felt that I was bringing her news of the official beginning of the publishing project.

As we wound our way through the increasingly hilly countryside, the drive took on a rare soothing quality for me, as if our mission was giving me a safe place in the storm of my grief.

We pulled into Erin, and I thought, "Now this is quaint central." Walking into the shop/home of Tim and Elke Inkster was like walking back in time. The floors were beautiful dark wood that creaked at precisely the right pitch. The place was crammed with printing, binding, and cutting machinery, which, though I had little knowledge of the trade, I could tell were very old. With just a look between us, Cheryl and I acknowledged to each other that we had come to exactly the right place. By the time we finished our meeting with Tim and Elke, we were as excited and happy as our deteriorated condition would permit.

Tim and Elke had many wonderful ideas and suggestions over the next several months. They helped us choose a beautiful Zephyr Antique Laid paper and brilliantly included images of a few of Stacey's poems as she had actually handwritten them. This added a wonderful personal and intimate quality to the book and inspired the last sentence in our Foreword: "This book contains many of her poems and when you finish reading them, you will know Stacey."

As the book evolved from idea to reality, we had to come up with a title and a cover design. The latter came first, decided on in a heartbeat. We chose to feature on the cover a picture of Stacey that she had taken of herself at the base of Mount Iztaccihuatl (Mt. Ixta is its short name) in central Mexico, the spring before her death.

Stacey had attended an Outward Bound course in British Columbia in August 1994 and had fallen in love with mountains and climbing. She wanted nothing more than to climb again. Having heard that a group of girls from Bishop Strachan School in Toronto were going to climb mountains in Mexico at March break 1995, she asked me if she could go. It was pretty much a rhetorical question; she knew that I always supported her and her sisters in any experience or activity that expanded their minds, skills, or physical wellbeing. I was not only happy to say yes, I also admired the fact that she was self-confident enough to join a group of complete strangers on such an adventure.

The picture shows Stacey standing with arms raised in a triumphant pose atop a large rock with the setting sun directly behind her. She appears as a silhouette, and you cannot tell from the photo whether she is facing the camera or the setting sun. All the girls tried to capture the setting sun that way, but only Stacey managed it. She was excited about the picture and had it enlarged and hung in her room. Stacey had not only given us the contents of the book, but the cover as well.

The title was more difficult to arrive at, as I'm told it often is with a book. The task is to convey, in very few words, the book's essence. In the end, with Tim and Elke's help, we landed on *I Am a Rose*, the title of Stacey's first poem.

I arrived home one evening a few months into the book's preparation. As was often the case with Cheryl in those days, she was in our bedroom with the lights out. I so wished I could take away her pain, but no one had that power. When I went into my home office, I noticed a couple of pieces of paper lying face down on my desk. I turned them over and saw that it was a poem Cheryl had written. I read the title, "Holding On." Then I read the poem, with great difficulty. The yearning for Stacey, the soul-devouring ache present in every word, were almost too much for me. I had to put the poem down from time to time as I read it, not only to wipe my eyes but also, as if distancing myself from a fierce fire, to get away from the poem's extreme intensity.

Holding On

I remember feeling your life inside me while I
   carried and nurtured you in my womb for nine
   months.
I'm holding on

I remember when you burst into the world, a part
   of me, and once again I marveled at the miracle
   of birth and the creation of life.
I'm holding on

I remember feeling your warmth as I cradled you
   in my arms and nursed you at my breast for nine
   months.
I'm holding on

I remember you as a lively little girl, your energy
   passing through me as I held you on my lap.
I'm holding on

As you grew, I watched with pride and love that
   special bond formed with sisters.
I'm holding on

I remember comforting you late into the night as
   your legs ached from growing pains.
 I'm holding on

Sometimes you needed consoling after coming to
   the end of a sad book like *Charlotte's Web*. I
   remember and,

I'm holding on

I experienced, with you, some of life's frustrations
and disappointments, but mostly it was your
personal challenges and your accomplishments
that I remember.
I'm holding on

I watched in amazement your vitality, grace,
strength, and agility while you participated in
gymnastics, ballet, jazz, swimming, tennis,
soccer, football, skiing, scuba diving, tae kwon
do, rock climbing, rollerblading, biking, aerobics, weight training, and jogging.
I'm holding on

I was in awe of your beauty — your bushy blond
hair, sparkling blue eyes, and dimpled smile. I
admired your creative and inquisitive mind, and
your great love of life.
I'm holding on

I observed your compassion and sensitivity when
you helped your friends and family members.
I'm holding on

I thrived on your hugs and kisses; your love notes;
your compliments and words of encouragement
to me; your inspiring poetry.
I'm holding on

Memories keep flashing through my mind, pulling

me in and out of reality: family vacations in
Florida or Mexico, family ski trips together,
those special family times at the cottage, and all
of your life cycle celebrations.
I'm holding on

I remember with horror receiving the news of your
  sudden accident and instant death, and not
  being there to hold you, to comfort you, to tell
  you how much I love you.
I'm trying to hold on

I remember with shock and disbelief seeing you for
  the last time at your funeral — my precious
  daughter lying still — no life.
I don't want to hold on

I remember with anguish kissing you goodbye:
  feeling your coldness next to my lips, and
  desperately wanting to hold you — to keep you.
  Part of me died and was buried with you.
I can't hold on

I remember feeling the outpouring of love and
  sensing the intense pain of family and friends
  when they came to say goodbye to you and to
  support us in this living nightmare.
I'm barely holding on

I remember, with unbearable pain, the expressions
  of torment on your father's and sisters' faces as
  you were lowered into the ground and then we

were driven home — leaving you behind.
I'm somehow still holding on

I remember, with confusion, poring over the details
    in the Accident Report and repeatedly reading
    "VSA/vital signs absent."
I wanted your pain to be my pain.
I'm still trying to hold on

I remember visiting you on Sundays — kneeling
    down beside your gravesite, my rational mind
    not comprehending what my eyes were seeing.
    Through a wall of tears, I focused and read the
    marker, "Stacey Levitt — August 30, 1995."
I don't want to hold on anymore

As I sit on your bed, in your undisturbed room, I
    cling to the memory of the sound of your voice,
    in laughter and in anger, with your family and
    your friends. The silence is now deafening.
I'm holding on

I remember the terrifying darkness each night and
    the incredible longing to hold you, and when
    morning finally arrives, you are still not here. I
    could never have imagined a loss so enormous
    — a pain so profound.
I'm holding on

I remember with anger, the unfairness of your
    being robbed of a full life and ask myself over
    and over again — why?

In my loneliness and fear, I will continue to
remember and to hold on to every precious
moment of your life. I can no longer hold you in
my arms, but I will cherish and hold your love
and warmth in my heart and in my mind forever.
I will never let go! You are part of me.

Love always, Mommy
February, 1996

Cheryl came into my office. My sobbing must have woken
her.

"This is wonderful, Cheryl!" I told her.

She said nothing, just looked at me, almost serenely.

"It has to go into Stacey's book!"

"I didn't write it for the book, Ned. I wrote it for myself
and for you and the girls."

"I understand, but it is too important to leave out."

Cheryl thought about it for a while. "Okay, if that is what
you want," she said.

I was now positive that the book would end with Cheryl's
poem and contributions from Marni, Jacqueline, and me.
Marni wrote her poem fairly quickly, but I was getting worried
as I waited for Jacqueline to write hers. Time was passing, but
I was afraid of putting her under too much pressure. She did
not disappoint me.

August 30, 1995: A Date to Remember
The police officer sat me and my parents down
in our living room and said that the young
woman who was hit by the car had succumbed
to her injuries… The events of the night of

August 30th play over and over every day in my head. It never gets easier. Everywhere I look, every room in my house, my school, her friends, and her boyfriend; all remind me of Stacey. Sometimes I even think that I see her walking through the halls at school — but she's not there anymore.

When Stacey died I not only lost my sister but I lost my friend and a role model. I love you Stacey, now and forever.

> Here I lie, sore and tired,
> Eyes closed and body limp.
> Pain and sorrow soar through me
> Like a flying eagle looking for its prey.
> I reach to stand up, but don't succeed.
> My soul floats away like the morning sun.
> I fall to the floor with no feeling left,
> I think to myself the force is too great.
> I should let go and flee from the earth.
> — JACQUELINE LEVITT

> In loving memory
> Of the most wonderful woman
> I know — my sister,
> Stacey Ellen Levitt.

As the publication date in May grew nearer, I began to have serious doubts about the project. I wondered if it would be seen as just a maudlin exercise in self-pity on my part. I wondered if people would just smile and take it when offered, but not actually ever read it. Tim assured me that, while it was not a Margaret Atwood poetry book, the book was lovely and touching and, for its intended purpose, magnificent.

The day we returned to Erin to pick up the first order of books, I was surprised by what I saw when I walked into the shipping room of Porcupine's Quill. As I looked at the eleven boxes of books that we were going to take home with us, I saw that someone had chosen to mark each box with our last name, "Levitt," and one word from the title of the book. Given that there was only one other order stored in the shipping room, our last name would have sufficed to identify the books. But each box was marked "Rose Levitt." This was my father's deceased mother's name.

We left Erin with the boxes in the back of our car, excited about delivering Stacey's books to our family and friends. We had decided to give a copy of the book to everyone who had contributed to the Stacey Levitt Athletic and Educational Fund or a charity of their own choosing. It would be our way of thanking them, and we had little doubt that they would appreciate the gesture. I harbored thoughts that the poetry book would be of interest to others, but I couldn't shake the apprehension that people would just humor us over the whole thing.

The list of donors was long and it took several days to address all the envelopes. Apparently, we committed two blunders on one envelope. We not only got the address of the recipient wrong, but we also forgot to place our return address on it. Several weeks later, we received a phone call from a worker at the post office.

"We could not deliver the package you sent, because the address was wrong," she told me. "We would normally have returned it to you, but there was no return address. As a result, our procedures require that we open the package and try and contact the sender."

"That is very kind of you. Thank you."

"Mr. Levitt, there is one more thing… Could you please tell me where I might buy two copies of the book?"

I told her that we weren't selling them, but that I would send her two copies. I took her address and hung up. Cheryl had been listening to the conversation from my end and pretty much knew what had just transpired. We looked at each other in amazement.

This was no isolated incident. We began to receive letter after letter from people thanking us for the gift and going on at length on how much the poetry, and Stacey's life, had touched them.

Now that I was confident in the strength of Stacey's book, I was hooked. We had written in the covering letter that Stacey was still having an impact on our world through her poetry. I grasped every appropriate opportunity to give a copy of the book to someone. As the book moved beyond our circle of family and friends, the reactions became even more intense and more healing for me. To know that Stacey's book brought comfort to other grieving families salvaged something positive for me from the tragedy and helped me each time I was fortunate enough to receive a letter of thanks.

Perhaps the greatest appreciation of the book is shown by those who give their copy away. This has happened several times. Invariably, it is done to help soothe someone in extreme pain and difficulty. One day I received a beautiful letter from a twenty-one-year-old woman in London, England, expressing her appreciation of Stacey's poetry and her own grief at losing her sixteen-year-old sister. The sister, like Stacey, had been struck and killed by a car. I communicated with the young woman, both to help her in any way I could and also out of curiosity as to how Stacey's book had traveled across an ocean to help another grieving person. I learned that an acquaintance in Toronto, who was from London, had given her copy of the book to a different family grieving the death of a teenage boy. As it happened, the boy's family lived on the same street in London. They had offered it to the girl's family when the sixteen-year-old died.

Teenagers relate very much to Stacey's poetry. She was one of them, and her poetry speaks thoughts and emotions so common to teenagers, but so difficult for most of them to express. One day, in the early spring of 1997, I was headed up Highway 400, alone, to attend to some matters at the cottage. As I was driving, I spotted a young man in his late teens. I have a policy of never picking up hitchhikers, but there was something about him — or maybe something about me, having journeyed along such a difficult path for almost two years by then — that made me feel it would be okay. I eased the car onto the shoulder of the highway and watched in the rearview mirror as he slowly jogged towards my car. He was polite and neatly dressed for a traveling teenager. I asked where he was headed.

"To Lafontaine," he said.

"You're in luck," I told him. "I am going to Thunder Beach and can take you right there." Lafontaine is no more than a good bike ride away from Thunder Beach.

We proceeded to engage in easy conversation. He was as much of a talker as I. He had been traveling after finishing high school and was returning home. Eventually, our conversation got around to the Outward Bound program and climbing mountains. He was fascinated by my stories of Stacey's Outward Bound trip to British Columbia and of her sudden death. After I pulled into the driveway of his home in Lafontaine, I reached into the glove compartment of my car, where I always carry two of Stacey's books, and gave him one. A week later, I received a long and friendly letter from him, which included these words:

> Thank you more than those words can say for sharing your treasure of Stacey with me. Thank her even more than you for being all she was, all she is, to me, to you, to anyone and everyone that knew her, to anyone and everyone that will ever taste the beauty that was her life. Thank you for being the seed, thank you for the inspiration. Thank Stacey.

Over the years I was a regular at one of my client's annual boys' golf weekends. Those who attended were real guys and great guys. That first summer after Stacey's accident, I took several copies of her book to the golf weekend. Dan, a Harley Davidson–riding, fun-loving man's man, took a copy and was not seen for several hours. When he rejoined the group, his eyes were red and his mood somber. As the weekend wound up, Dan asked if I would send him a couple more copies of the book, as there was something he wanted to make for me. He said he did not want to explain what he was planning. I obliged him, without giving it much thought.

Dan called me about a month later and invited me over to his office. When I entered his office, Bob, our host for the boys' weekend, was with him. He gestured to a package on the table and invited me to open it. As I unwrapped it, the first thing that caught my eye was the picture of Stacey we used for the back flap of her book. It was centered on a beautiful burgundy leather box. On the box, engraved with gold letters, was the title *I Am a Rose*. I opened the box gently. Inside was a book bound in the same burgundy leather. The style was that of what a rare book collector would treasure. Dan, whose family was in the book binding business, had taken Stacey's book apart and had rebound it exquisitely. He had even had the pages edged in gold.

I needed several minutes to regain my composure to thank him in a way the gesture deserved. My family and I began a tradition of reading Stacey's poetry from this book at holiday meals.

We were coming up on the first anniversary of Stacey's death. A great deal of emphasis is placed on the first year following the death of a loved one. Common advice is to refrain from making any major changes in your life until the end of the first year. Grief is at its most intense for parents and family in the first year as you experience every annual event for the first time without your child: their birth date, your birth date, holidays, Mother's Day, Father's Day.

I witnessed Cheryl sinking lower in the days approaching the first Mother's Day and, as the first Father's Day approached, I was sliding into the same kind of depressed state. Then something happened to soften the blow of that day. Over that first year, Marni had created inspiring messages of hope for Cheryl and me using pictures of Stacey. She enlarged the picture of Stacey on a mountain in British Columbia, during her Outward Bound program, and added a message to reflect Stacey's strength and courage. She also made a Calendar of Hope for Cheryl. Each month contained a picture of Stacey alone or with her sisters and a note or a quotation from Marni.

We kept dozens of family pictures on our piano and buffet in the dining room. These pictures were Marni's raw materials for her mother's calendar, and, as it turned out, for her gift to me.

"Dad, look what I found by accident," Marni said. It was Father's Day and she was holding a sparkling picture of Stacey in a tie-dyed T-shirt, and a piece of yellow paper. The piece of paper had been given to me by Stacey several years before on Father's Day and had been stuck in the frame of this picture. Marni found it when choosing that picture for her gift to me. On the paper was written:

> Dearest Daddy,
> I love you so much and I can't begin to tell you all you've done for me. What would I do if I didn't have someone to hug?
>
> I love you so much (and the new video camera too).
>
> With lots and lots of love,
> Your loving daughter,
> Stacey
>
> Papa je t'aime avec tout mon coeur. Qu'est-ce-que je ferais sans toi?
> XOXOXOXOXOXO

In May of the first year after Stacey's death, a colleague at work was cleaning out a file of telephone messages and realized he had not given me a message from shortly after Stacey's accident. It was from a young woman, Cheri. The message said that she had been at the scene of the accident and wished to speak to me. I got in touch with her, and eventually Cheryl and I had her over to the house.

Cheri turned out to be a beautiful young woman whose interests were very much like Stacey's. Just as Stacey had loved martial arts and scuba diving, Cheri had a black belt in karate and had trained as a rescue diver. She had also trained in emergency first aid, specifically to help in traffic accidents.

Cheri told us that she had come upon the accident scene moments after Stacey was hit. Her training led her to park her car as a barrier to oncoming traffic, to protect Stacey. She approached Stacey and put a blanket on her. Cheri was not emotionally prepared for this accident. She knew right away that Stacey's injuries were fatal, but stayed with her, gently stroking her and speaking encouraging words to her until the ambulance arrived. She told us that Stacey did not suffer.

When we discovered, during that meeting, that Cheri rented diving equipment on her diving trips, we offered her Stacey's gear, which was only slightly used. Cheri was too emotional to accept the equipment, but after our meeting realized that it would help me if she accepted the gift. Later she thanked me with a letter from Australia, where she had used the equipment for the first time. She knew, from our conversations, that Stacey had planned to go to Australia after finishing high school at the end of December and had planned for me to meet her there to dive the Great Barrier Reef.

Not only does the bereaved family emphasize the first year of grief, but everyone around you assumes that by the close of the first year you should have finished grieving and should be ready to resume your life. Nothing could be further from the truth. In some ways, I was feeling worse because the expected relief did not materialize. What could I do now?

Ben, a bereaved father, had told me about how he climbed Mount Kilimanjaro with his deceased son's coach whistle. He described the climb and blowing the whistle at the top of the mountain as cathartic. I looked at the picture of Stacey on Mt. Ixta. I read the entry from the journal she kept on that trip:

> Day 5, Wed. March 15, 1995
> Here I sit on a rock 12,000 feet up at the
> base of Mt. Ixta. I'm bundled in eight layers
> of clothing, watching the sun set through
> low-lying clouds while a few light snowflakes
> drift on the wind. It's beautiful up here.
> Rolling hills with large tufts of grass and
> trees, with grazing bulls that have definitely
> left their mark. There is a storm at the top
> of Ixta that may prevent us from climbing it.
> I've decided that I have to give it a try. I will
> set my mind and soul to it but I will also
> prepare myself for possible disappointment.
> I want to do this more than anything. I have
> to learn to suffer discomfort. If I succeed I
> will feel great and if I try I'll feel great, but if
> I stay back I'll never know! My hands are
> now too cold to write so I will hope for the
> best and end this entry with a promise to try.

Her expedition was indeed not able to complete the balance of the climb of Mt. Ixta the following day because of stormy weather conditions. I looked at her book. I knew what I had to do next.

CHAPTER SIX

sleeping woman

The first rays of light begin to glow,
I have found the flaming ring of gold.
The time has come; I now must go.
I have the power; it's mine to hold.
Mirror, mirror on the wall,
I'll be there soon, I hear your call.
As I float up, the sun's rays pass me by.
I smile, for my home is now in the sky.
Shattered glass on the floor,
mirror, mirror there is no more.
FROM "RING OF FIRE," STACEY LEVITT, 1990

"FRANK, I THINK I AM GOING TO FINISH STACEY'S CLIMB UP Mt. Ixta," I told my brother on one of my many phone calls to him.

"I will come with you, Ned."

"You will?"

"I wouldn't want it any other way."

I thought all the sacrifices Frank had made to support me during the first year were enough. Taking the time, spending the money, and enduring the challenge of high-altitude climbing seemed way beyond the call of duty. But I was delighted that he would be by my side.

I had never climbed before, and I did not know where to start. How do you get to Mt. Ixta? When is the best time of year to climb? What gear should be taken? These and several other questions needed answering.

I phoned Chris, who had led the expedition that Stacey had been on. After telling her who I was and what I wanted to do, I asked her for the information I thought I needed.

"Have you ever climbed at high altitude, Ned?" she asked.

"No. In fact, I have never climbed mountains at all."

After a worried pause, she said, "Ned, I think there is a lot more you need to know. Climbing Mt. Ixta is not a walk in the park." She went on to tell me about a friend of hers, Scott Kress, who was an experienced climber and Toronto-based Outward Bound instructor. He had climbed Mt. Ixta several times. She would speak to him for me.

Scott turned out to be very sensitive to what I wanted to do. He was going to climb Mt. Ixta with three friends, Murdo, Collin, and Collin's wife, Alex, in the middle of November and would be pleased to have Frank and me join their expedition. I sent him a copy of Stacey's book, and we made arrangements to meet and start planning the trip.

The first meeting was at my house. Scott, his long dark hair tied back in a ponytail, had an air of serenity and calm. He chose his words carefully and seemed absolutely confident and in control. As I came to know him better, I realized that his quiet confidence was a product of having survived the many challenges he had faced in his insatiable desire to touch the sky from the tops of mountains. All of this was in stark contrast to the bundle of uncertainty and confusion that was me.

After the usual pleasantries, we got down to business.

"Ned, I think you should know that less than half the people who try to climb Mt. Ixta succeed on their first attempt," Scott told me. "It's not that it's such a technical climb. You don't need ropes and pitons. But it is 17,000 feet, and that altitude is a major factor. Also, the weather can be very unpredictable. We have to plan well and, if we do, we will increase our chances of success."

Scott wasn't fooling around. He told me that every year one or two people either die or are severely injured on Mt. Ixta. On the mountain, everyone was responsible for each other's safety. He wanted to make sure my brother and I were prepared to make the commitment necessary to climb.

The challenge and danger of the climb became even more real when Scott pulled a release form from his bag, which he insisted that I sign and have Frank sign before we went any further. There was no hesitation on my part or Frank's. Frank, in fact, when I told him about Scott's concerns, was even more committed to accompanying me, because he was worried about my mental and physical state. As far as I was concerned, the climb was a mission for Stacey; if I died in attempting it, I would be with her again.

We had only a few weeks to pull everything together, but I was dealing with a professional. Scott gave us lists of required clothing and equipment and a draft agenda for the climb. He helped us procure the more specialized climbing equipment, but I had to buy or borrow enough clothing to outfit not only me but Frank as well — as a Floridian, he owned nothing warmer than a windbreaker.

The agenda included entries for time on the expedition to learn new skills, such as walking with crampons through the snow and ice, manoeuvring while roped to each other, and the technique for using your ice axe to stop a slide down the mountain. This last skill was particularly important. We would be roped together with the other climbers, and one person's uncontrolled slide could end the lives of the whole team.

Feeling confident that I was in good hands for the physical aspects of the climb, I began to think about the emotional, symbolic, and spiritual aspects of what I was about to do. I told Frank that if we made it to the summit, I wanted to perform a service for Stacey there. He agreed and said we should both think of some appropriate things to read and say. We could work on the service when we met up in Mexico City before the climb. We also agreed that we would both keep journals of the trip, as Stacey had. I had already decided to laminate the picture of Stacey that we kept on our refrigerator and leave it at the summit, along with a copy of *I Am a Rose.*

There were only a few days left before I was to fly to Mexico City. I was going to meet Frank there, stay the night, and then we would join Scott, Collin, Alex, and Murdo at Amecameca, the small town at the base of the mountain. How could I leave the book on the mountain with some chance that it would survive for a little while at least? My thoughts ran to purchasing a box that would protect it. I could chain the box to the mountain to secure it from the elements and keep it in one place. I wanted to place a message on the box so people would know what was inside and why it was put there.

What kind of box should it be? I scoured the Yellow Pages for companies that might have a box that would work, without luck. Frank suggested that I have it made, but I didn't know who could make it, especially in the short time we had before we were to leave. I opened the Yellow Pages again and searched its index. My eyes fell on the category "boat building." Of course. Boats are built to withstand the worst of weather conditions. I saw an advertisement for a company on Lakeshore Boulevard and went there the next morning on my way to the office.

The man behind the counter was about my age. He looked at me patiently as I cast about trying to explain what I needed.

"So let me understand what you want," he said. "You need a box that will contain a book, and the box will be affixed to the side of a mountain in Mexico. So it has to have holes in it for pitons or chains. But it also has to have a lid and a latch, but won't be locked, because you want people to open the lid and read the book. Have I got that right?"

"Yes, and I will have to have a permanent sign on the box telling people what's inside."

"How big is the book?"

I pulled a copy from my briefcase and handed it to him. As he looked at the cover, read the excerpt from Stacey's journal on the flap and some of the poems, his mood changed dramatically. He looked up with eyes starting to tear and said, "I understand completely what you are trying to do. My teenage son died three years ago. These last three years have been like being in prison."

He made the box in three days. He said he had made it blue like the sky. He refused to take any money for it. It was constructed from the molded fiberglass that is used in boat building and had sturdy hinges and a shiny stainless steel latch of the type you would see on an expensive yacht. He had installed a gasket around the opening to keep the elements out.

The next hurdle was to have a sign made for the top of the box telling the world what was inside. With time nearly gone, I went to a trophy maker, who suggested that we do a simple sign on top under clear acrylic and another sign on the inside of the lid. The top sign said, in English and Spanish, "In loving Memory of Stacey Levitt, Our Daughter, Our Sister, Our Friend, 1977–1995." The sign on the inside of the lid, which would be readily visible when the lid was open, would read, again in English and Spanish, "After reading this copy of Stacey's book, please leave it for others to experience. Copies are available by writing to the Levitt family at…"

The box was finally ready the day before I was set to leave for Mexico. That night, I spread out, in Marni's now unoccupied room, everything I was taking on the trip. I went through the checklists Scott had provided. Everything seemed to be in order. The sign on the top of the box was white with black lettering, and I had purchased a white plastic chain to affix it to the mountain. I liked the look of the chain, but more importantly, it was light and would be easy to carry up the mountain. I knew that the plastic would not last anywhere close to as long as a metal chain, but I did not think the box would last on the mountain for very long anyway. Even one day on the mountain, so some climbers might come across it and read Stacey's poetry, would be enough for me.

The box was structurally sound and beautiful, but it was far bigger than the book. The book did not look right lying so far down in it. I searched the house for something that would prop the book up attractively. Down in the furnace room, where we store all kinds of useless things, including boxes from past purchases, I spotted a box that had contained the Walkman Stacey was wearing at the time of the accident.

This took me back to the day I received her personal effects from the police. They had given me a plastic bag with very little in it. No clothing was in the bag, for obvious reasons. However, her running shoes were there, which, despite someone's attempt to clean them, still had remnants of her blood on them. But it was her Walkman that had cascaded me into a black pit of anguish. I could not believe how shattered the earphones were. I remembered having bought the best ones on the market for her. They curved around her ears to make them more secure and comfortable, and the earpieces fitted snugly into her ears for good sound. The cord had a volume control switch for easy access. As I looked at the demolished earphones, with the earpieces dangling at the end of exposed wires, I could feel the impact of the car.

Now I looked inside the box and found the charcoal grey packing foam that contained the Walkman when it was purchased. The Walkman had nestled in a hollowed out square in the middle of the foam pad. I could not believe how perfectly it fit, as if custom-made. Stacey's book now sat up higher in the box and, with the charcoal foam pad, made for quite an attractive presentation. When I lifted the book out of the box, I pondered the hollow where the Walkman had sat. Something needed to be placed in it. I looked around Marni's room and my eyes fell on a thick little notepad. It was deep purple, Stacey's favorite colour, and its pages were a beautiful unbleached and rustic ivory colour. As I placed it into the hollow, which was exactly the right size, I knew that the box was almost ready. One last touch. I put two pens into the box for climbers who might want to write in response to reading the book.

When I showed Jacqueline the box, she said, "Stacey gave that pad to Marni when she came back from Mexico!" I stared at the pad in the box for a while and then said, "Well, it's going back to Mexico with me."

Scott and I communicated almost daily on the lead-up to the trip, either by fax, telephone, or e-mail. I wrote to him that I was planning to perform a service if we made it to the summit. He replied with a wonderful suggestion. He said he knew of some native traditions around loss and grieving. "One is that you take some food or something symbolic regarding the deceased and cast it into the wind or river so that it is carried to their spirit and into nature." In a flash I decided to take the petals of eighteen red roses to throw to the wind at the top of Mt. Ixta.

Scott went on to mention that he sometimes did amateur documentary filming on his climbs. Would I mind it if he filmed our trip? He had even lined up someone who might be interested in producing a documentary about what we were doing. I told him I would think about that.

It did not take long before I told Scott that he was free to film our trip. In fact, it not only would give me a memento of the trip, but it might also capture something of value for other bereaved parents. However, I was concerned that the process of filming might detract from what I needed to do personally. After giving it some thought, I decided to write out some notes for the filming and a mission statement for each objective. The following is what I wrote and distributed to everyone going on the expedition.

Notes for Filming the Climb to the Summit of Mt. Ixta, Nov. 15th to Nov. 21st, 1996

Introduction & Mission Statements

I felt it would be helpful to put some of my thoughts on paper concerning the filming on our expedition. Above all, this is a very important personal mission for me and another step along my path to finding some peace and solace after losing Stacey. While I am enthusiastic about the possibility of creating an interesting and perhaps useful film, I must resist the temptation to get too involved in the direction and content of the filming and therefore "lose the moment." So I felt, by committing some of my thoughts and ideas to paper and sharing them with the other members of the expedition, I would then be able to step back and let it simply happen. With luck, the camera will become just another member of our group and events will unfold naturally.

My Mission Statement for the Trip

I will climb to the top of Mt. Ixta for my daughter Stacey, who wanted so very much to reach its summit, but, due to circumstances beyond her control, could not complete the climb. I will experience some of what she did in March of 1995 and will feel more in touch with her spirit every step along the way. This climb will be a tribute to her and to her strength and courage. I will leave a copy of her wonderful book of poems behind for others to experience, which will help to perpetuate her memory and bring her legacy to other climbers who may share her love of the mountains, zest for life, and the thrill of personal challenge.

Mission Statement for the Film
The pain and devastation that a parent experiences after losing a child is profound. A parent never "recovers"; you simply try and build a different life around the loss. Everyone who survives (and not all do), finds their own unique path to the resolution of their grief. What works for one parent will not work for another. However, experience has shown that grief can be diminished when it is shared. The purpose of this film will be to share my grief over the loss of Stacey; to demonstrate that you can survive such a loss; to show the value of taking action and memorialization in the process of coping with extreme grief; and to illustrate the value of "trekking" when you are seeking personal growth and insight.

Themes

There are a number of themes that can be explored in this filming, for example:

- Loss is part of life, but our culture does not deal well with the issues around loss.
- The importance of relationships in resolving grief, i.e., my brother was by my side throughout my ordeal and is climbing by my side now.
- The interplay of personal physical challenge and the challenge of dealing with grief.
- The relationship of parent and child, before and after death.

Possible Title of the Film

"I Am a Rose: A Journey Through Grief."

Cheryl drove me to Toronto's Pearson Airport on Thursday, November 14, at 6:00 p.m. for a 7:40 flight to Mexico City. We said a tearful goodbye. I was torn about leaving her alone, but I needed to do this, and she knew how important the trip was for me.

Sitting in the departure lounge, alone with my thoughts, I picked up my journal, turned to the first blank page, and wrote:

Thursday, Nov. 14/96 7:00 p.m.

I am sitting at the gate waiting to board my flight to Mexico City. Cheryl & I said good-bye & she cried. My heart aches for her & all her pain.

I have never kept a journal before & I am uncertain about what to write. But Stacey has taught me many things and one is the power and importance of keeping a journal for important trips and events. I love all her journals and wish there were more. I long for her so much.

I am excited and at the same time apprehensive. While the trip has been very well planned, I really don't know what awaits me on Mt. Ixta. I am aware that I am "searching" for Stacey, but I have no choice right now. If she were here she would have taken this trip with me. I feel her spirit beside me & I pray that she is in a good place.

The four-hour flight went uneventfully. It was wonderful to see Frank at the airport in Mexico City. He had arrived first and had already checked into the Marriot hotel attached to the airport. We hugged each other firmly and for a long time. It was good to have each other on this voyage into the unknown.

After redistributing the various pieces of clothing and equipment we had for each other, we ate a late snack of energy bars and trail mix and went to bed.

There was no need for alarm clocks. We were both up very early the next day, partly because of excitement and partly because of the mild headaches the altitude produced. Mexico City sits at about 7,000 feet above sea level; we only had 10,000 feet more to go.

Before we arrived in Mexico City, Frank had a business associate arrange a car and driver. After a hardy buffet breakfast of eggs, bacon, pancakes, and an assortment of buns, we set out with our driver to navigate the treacherous Mexico City traffic. It was a brilliantly sunny day with atypically low pollution levels. As we left the city, the arid scrubland of rural Mexico emerged. In the city, we had passed by stalls of merchants and beggars everywhere. In the countryside, we saw many tiny eateries along the road but no beggars. The character of the people changed the farther we drove. In the city, it was all hustle and bustle and what can you do for me? In the countryside, I began to experience the incredible warmth and generosity of the Mexican people.

As we pulled into Amecameca an hour and a half later, I realized that I was seeing a side of Mexico I never knew existed. To that time, I had only known its cities and resorts. This town of a couple of thousand souls contained a permanent farmers' market occupying half the town square, with many different farm products and goods, and food stalls every few feet. There were bright clothing, kites, and streamers everywhere I looked. It was Friday afternoon, and many people had come from the countryside to the town to trade their goods and enjoy a festive weekend.

After a short hunt, we found Scott, Collin, Alex, and Murdo in the town square. I very quickly realized that these were special people. Their Outward Bound training made them perfect leaders and companions. They were eager to know more about us, Stacey, and what we wanted to accomplish. As we sat around the monument to a hero of the

Mexican revolution, Scott filmed while I answered questions about the purpose of our trip.

Scott had made reservations for us at a local no-star hotel. He had said there really was not much to choose from, but he had done his best, in the price range Outward Bound people could afford. One thing good about the accommodations: there were no rats. Apparently, the hotel was so bad, the rats would not stay there. As for the shower, you had to run around in it to get wet. And the towels and sheets were made from recycled sandpaper. However, I was pleasantly surprised by how easy it was to get a tasty and cheap meal in town. In every restaurant, it was like eating in someone's home. They made you feel like an honored guest and were so happy when you said you liked the food.

We were now 3,000 feet higher than Mexico City, and our reactions to the altitude were increasing: more frequent and painful headaches, shortness of breath, and a slight feeling of nausea. We decided to take cabs up to Paso de Cortes the next day and hike along the road three or four miles to La Joya, the point beyond which cars can no longer travel. We would then hike back to Paso de Cortes and return to Amecameca. Scott felt the exposure to higher altitude and then rest would help us acclimatize before our climb.

As we sped along in the cabs the next day, after an 8 a.m. breakfast of bread and cheese and bottled water, I was aware that I was seeing everything through Stacey's eyes. We were luckier, though, with warmer and sunnier weather than she had experienced. But I knew she had gone through the same preparations to climb. At one point, I noticed that the cab driver had a red rose on a wet towel on the floor between the two front seats. It was there for good luck, he said.

Chris, who had led Stacey's climb, had told me that the

picture of Stacey had been taken at La Joya. When we got there, I took out Stacey's book and began to search for the rock that she was standing on when the picture was taken. Since it was the weekend, La Joya, in reality a campground, was very busy, with many families camping and cooking there. Some had modern tents, but more made shelter out of plastic sheeting or slept in their trucks. The mood was as festive and happy as any resort in the world, or maybe more so. Eventually, I saw two rocks on the periphery of the campground that seemed to answer to the photo on the cover of Stacey's book. As I stood there, holding the book away from me in my right hand, a Mexican man approached. He introduced himself as Miguel and asked what I was trying to do. My Spanish was nonexistent but his English was pretty good. I was happy we could talk.

"My daughter had this picture taken of her in March 1995 on one of these rocks," I told him. "I am trying to figure out which one it was."

Miguel, an engineer from Mexico City, said he came to La Joya all the time to climb, and he would help me. He took the book and examined the cover. After a short while, he pointed to the larger rock and said it was the one. He showed me how some of the landmarks matched up, like the rock outcropping in the background of the photo, which he said was called "The Saint," because, with a little imagination, it resembled a priest praying.

Miguel asked me if he could look at the book. I left it with him and went to stand on the rock where Stacey had stood, to see what she must have seen. We were at 12,000 feet, higher than I had ever been outside of an airplane. Intertwining slopes and valleys fell away from where I was standing. Behind me were the soaring, jagged peaks of Mt. Ixta. The sheer size and magnitude of the place made you feel small but at the same time protected. These mountains have been there for many centuries, while man has come and gone. How important could anyone's problems be in a place like this? Now I could understand the power captured in the photograph.

When I returned to Miguel, he was holding the book to his chest and wiping his eyes. I told him what our plans were, and he said he must bring his seventeen-year-old daughter, Isadora, here to meet me. I thought he was making an idle comment. I did not realize that he was going to return to Mexico City that very moment to get her.

We returned to Amecameca around 4 in the afternoon to make plans for the next day. Going higher and then returning to lower altitudes was helping me adjust, and I was starting to feel better. Scott said the great weather was a mixed blessing. "We need the snow to melt for drinking water and it will be a more dangerous climb on the summit bid without snow to dig into with our crampons." He added, though, that climbing plans had to be flexible to deal with the unexpected, which you could expect on every climb.

The next day was spent purchasing additional provisions and lots of extra drinking water. Water is necessary not just to quench your thirst, but to combat altitude sickness, which, as I was beginning to realize, was a force to be reckoned with. At La Joya, I was increasingly nauseated and significantly shorter of breath. In the extreme, altitude can kill you by causing the blood vessels in your brain to rupture. Scott's plan was to establish a base camp at La Joya the next day and do several sorties partway up the mountain to cache water. These short climbs would further acclimatize us and make us less likely to get sick on the actual climb.

When we arrived at La Joya the next day, it was again sunny and warm. We found a perfect camping spot and made ourselves comfortable. Miguel came by and introduced us to his daughter. Isadora. We learned that she was a radio and television arts student in Mexico City. She was beautiful and sweet, with an inquisitive intelligence. Now I had another person who wanted to know all about Stacey and her adventures. She had already read, from cover to cover, the copy of Stacey's book that I had given to Miguel.

I asked Miguel, who knew the mountain in intimate detail, where he thought we might put the box. He made several suggestions but thought that the second pass would probably be best. I had quickly concluded that La Joya was not the right place, because there were too many people who came there just to party. The people who climbed from there were different and would more likely respect the box and the book.

That night I experienced real altitude sickness. My bowels had turned to stone, and my head ached. I couldn't eat and slept only in fits. It turns bitter cold at night in the mountains, below zero that time of year, and I fleetingly thought about turning back. I was no better the next morning. Nonetheless, as Stacey had said in her journal, I had "to learn to suffer discomfort." I knew she had felt similarly.

We selected our clothing and gear for the first climb. I packed lots of water, two liters, along with four copies of Stacey's book and the blue box. Miguel and Isadora joined us. We agreed to go as far as the second pass, about a four-hour hike (for gringos), before returning to base camp. I was told to move slowly, but nobody needed to remind me. As we started up the first steep trail, my head felt like it would explode. Breathing was very difficult. It felt like I was climbing steep stairs with a pillow over my face.

As the morning unfolded, it became increasingly sunny and warm. I could not imagine the climb with snow and cold weather, which was more normal for that time of year. At the first pass, I did not feel any worse, which I took to be a minor victory. There, we could see the nearby mountain called Popocteptl ("Popo," as it is called), which is an active volcano. Our mountain, Iztaccihuatl, was also volcanic. The two mountains' names are from the pre-Hispanic Nahuatl language. In mythology, Popo, a warrior, and the beautiful Ixta, the daughter of the chief, were in love. Before they could marry, Popo went off to war against another tribe. Some mischief makers reported to Ixta that Popo had been killed, which was not true. Ixta took her life because of her profound grief. On Popo's return, he, too, was overcome by grief and killed himself, but not before he had a magic spell cast over the two of them. Now Popo, with his plumes of white steam, stands guard over Ixta, the sleeping woman or woman at rest, which is what the name means in English. As you look at Mt. Ixta from a distance, you can clearly see the lines of a woman in repose. The first time I heard this, I remembered that Stacey's Hebrew name, Menucha, means "rest."

It was getting steeper and steeper as we proceeded. The next leg up, to the second pass, was frightening, at least for an inexperienced climber like me. We had to be sure to avoid climbing directly under someone else, because of the risks from falling rocks and stones dislodged by the higher climber. The last few feet up to the second pass were almost vertical, or so it seemed.

The pass created a large, open, flat space. Many people came this far to picnic before returning to the base of the mountain. The more adventurous camped here before continuing on to the more treacherous climbs and the summit.

On one side there was a spectacular view of Popo and on the other side a magnificent view of the rest of Ixta and the valleys below. Once I had recovered my breath, I knew this was where the book should go. Miguel and Scott both agreed. They reasoned that more people would take the time to look at Stacey's book here than at the summit, where climbers typically spend very little time before descending.

After a lunch of peanut butter sandwiches, we all headed down to base camp. While still dangerous, descending was a pleasure compared with the climb up. As we went lower in altitude, our ailments quickly abated. That night, I felt so much better. My appetite had returned and I slept soundly. Scott was obviously taking the right approach to preparing us.

The next morning we hiked back up to the second pass, with lots of water. Murdo and Collin climbed higher to scout out a place for our high camp, and to hide the water bottles we would need for the summit bid. While they were gone, Scott and I picked a spot on a rock face for the box. The box would be clearly visible from all directions and would be easily reached by a few rocks that acted like steps.

Before affixing the box to the rock face, I put three stones in it. One of the stones, which Cheryl had originally placed at Stacey's grave, had the picture of a dolphin on it (Stacey had a dolphin tattooed on her ankle). It is a Jewish custom to place a stone at a grave, when visiting, which echoes back to biblical times, when the accumulation of such stones over time became the marker for the grave. Another of the stones was brought by Frank from the ocean. The third was from Thunder Beach.

As we were busily working, a man named Tobin happened by. He was a Quaker from the U.S. on a mission in Mexico City and had recently lost a friend in a climbing accident. With his companions, he had intended to eat his lunch there and head back down the mountain. He inquired what we were doing. I took a moment to explain why I had come to Mt. Ixta and handed him a copy of Stacey's book to look at as we continued our work on the box. As we finished, I saw that he was engrossed in reading Stacey's poetry. Tears were slowly working their way down his face. Scott asked him to say a few words into the camera. Months later, the man wrote me to tell me that he loved to write poetry, but had stopped doing so until the encounter with our expedition.

I took the privilege of making the first entry in the notepad:

> I put this box with your book at this place so those people with strength and courage who pass this way will know you and know of your great strength and courage. I love you so deeply words are not enough and I had to express my love with deeds.
> — Daddy

One by one, Frank, Scott, Collin, Alex, Murdo, Miguel, and Isadora wrote messages to Stacey in the notepad. I then turned to Tobin, who had remained at the pass, fascinated and emotional about what we were doing, and asked him if he wanted to write something. He wrote:

> If death transforms us to a spirit which enters more deeply into the heart of those we have loved, then perhaps it is in death that we are fully known. And so we live on in the heart of another and the sharpness of death

slowly fades … I only know Stacey through the love of her father and through her words carefully chosen. It is enough. Stacey moves me.

— Tobin

Satisfied that the box was now in a good place, I was pleased we were heading down the mountain, back to La Joya, to eat, sleep, and prepare for what lay ahead.

CHAPTER SEVEN

closer to heaven

In my mind, dreams possess me.
Dreams of love and fairy tales,
of flowers, blue skies,
sunshine and rainbows.
What will become of me?
My friends?
The knowledge lies within
the unknown.
Only time will tell.

FROM "VISIONS," STACEY LEVITT, 1991

THE NEXT MORNING WE AWOKE AT AROUND 7 TO A BRILLIANTLY clear day. The morning cold seemed to evaporate more quickly this day, as the sun cleared the eastern ridge of Mt. Ixta. After a quick breakfast, our campsite hummed with activity. Tents had to be knocked down and packed tightly into their bags. We had to make decisions about what to leave behind in Collin's van, as we were now going to make a high camp, well above the tree line, from which our bid for the summit would be made. If an item would not keep us warm or help us climb, it remained in the van. We left behind all food that needed any type of preparation and took only enough of the rest to make it to the summit and back alive.

Miguel and Isadora had now become part of our expedition. In fact, by then, it seemed like they had been part of it from the beginning. Their presence was comforting. Miguel knew the mountain better than anyone. And Isadora was climbing with me as Stacey would have done. She stayed by me constantly, to make sure I was safe.

We were now used to the altitude we had reached. As we started up the first winding trail through the grass slope, onto the first ridge, I was full of excitement, anticipating seeing the box again. I paused and looked behind me to see a group of other campers, mostly Mexicans, waving at us. Word of what we were doing on Mt. Ixta had spread all over the mountain. Mexicans have a beautiful simplicity and generosity of heart, and our mission had touched them deeply.

We moved slowly, this time more because of our now heavier packs, but the path had become familiar, and the climb to the second pass was a pleasure.

I scrambled quickly over the last rocks leading to the second pass and almost sprinted to the box. I opened it and pulled out the notepad. Even in the short time since we had put the box in place, some climbers had opened it, respected Stacey's book, and left messages. I was gratified to read an entry from three climbers from the Czech Republic: "To the memory of Stacey Levitt." And Miguel translated an entry made in Spanish.

Stacey,

Now that you are a spirit, you understand the nature of humanity. Poor weather impeded you from reaching the peak of this beautiful mountain. Each time I go to the peak, I'll come by for you and take you with me.

Your friend now and forever,

D.H.H.

After a short rest, we turned our attention to the next leg of the journey. We started up a rocky slope to the north that helps define the second pass. As we were climbing up, a group of Mexican climbers was coming down the same slope. The eldest of the group stopped to chat with Miguel. Miguel led the man over to me and introduced us. He then told me that the man had just come back from the summit, and, while he was there he had dedicated his success in reaching the top to Stacey and had said a prayer for her. I felt a warmth spread throughout my body and hugged the man.

Our group continued climbing. Just before we disappeared over the top of the ridge, without consulting, all of us stopped, turned, and took one last look at the box. Collin was the only one who spoke. "With the white chains as limbs, the box, from this distance, looks like a climber scaling the rock face," he said. Everyone agreed.

Mt. Ixta is really a series of several volcanoes. Over many centuries, the lava has formed and reformed the landscape on the mountain. Unlike Popo, with its more traditional cone shape, Ixta is a fascinating array of large and small peaks, hidden valleys, sharp ridges, and surprises around every bend. The next stretch was a much harder climb than we had encountered thus far. As we moved higher, the altitude became a problem again, causing shortness of breath and requiring more frequent rests. At times, I found myself walking along too narrow a trail. My right shoulder brushed the mountain as I walked while off my left shoulder was a void: a steep drop off the cliff. Just when I thought I could take it no longer, we arrived at a spacious plateau and stopped for lunch.

Miguel was going to leave us at this point and return with Isadora to La Joya, but first he had a surprise for us. He had brought with him all the makings of a sumptuous repast to prepare us for the last part of the climb. In a flash he had several propane burners going, and frying pans and pots seemed to appear out of thin air. As he began to work, Isadora asked if she could interview me about Stacey for a radio project she was working on for school. We found a comfortable place away from the commotion of Miguel's kitchen.

Isadora listened intently to everything I had to say. I had brought with me from Toronto a copy of two audio tapes and a Walkman. One tape was Stacey's workout tape, which she had in her Walkman when she was hit, and one was a tape of her funeral. I was intending to listen to the workout tape as I climbed and the funeral tape when I reached the summit. As it turned out, I did not listen to either one. Isadora was eager to listen to them.

When we returned to the group, I could not believe what Miguel had created. There, shimmering before my eyes, was a banquet worthy of any good restaurant: a variety of pastas, some with cream sauce, some with tomato sauce, one with chicken, another with beef, yet another with just vegetables and an amazing mélange of wild mushrooms. My appetite returned long enough to stuff myself with this sumptuous lunch.

After hugs and farewells, the rest of us resumed our

climb, now into higher and even more intimidating terrain.

As we climbed, I recalled how, when I learned how to ski, the bunny hills seemed intimidating — until I attempted the steeper runs. Climbing was a lot like that. As I tried to keep my balance and my nerve on a scree slope that felt like it was at a ninety-degree angle, I longed for the earlier slopes that had challenged me at the beginning.

The surface of a scree slope is made up of a combination of sand and gravel. It is very soft and shifts dramatically as you try to get a firm foothold. The first time I stepped into the scree, I thought I was going to slide down to the bottom of a huge crevasse. Collin, Alex, and Murdo taught me the technique of making a foothold and letting the loose gravel and sand settle before attempting to put my full weight down.

The next challenge was a steep rock face. Here I had to fight the natural reflex of trying to hug the mountain. With difficulty, my teachers got me to stand more erect, so that more of the tread of my boots would be in contact with the surface of the rock. While this was counterintuitive to a frightened mind, it did indeed prove to be the safer way to climb.

And so it went until we reached 15,000 feet. It was about 4, and Scott decided that this was where we would make our high camp.

I asked Scott, with some concern, where we were going to pitch the tents. All I could see was a small ledge against the mountain and a steep scree slope falling away dramatically from the ledge. He muttered something about the mountain giving us some protection against the wind, and before I knew it the tents were up on the small ledge.

Now, at 15,000 feet, I was discovering another consequence of high altitude. I began to have difficulty finding my words and thoughts. Perhaps this was what a minor stroke might feel like. Another piece of reality hit with a thud, too: dinner was nothing like Miguel's lunch. It was made up of some nuts, dried fruit, and old bread. But that did not really matter to Frank or me. By this point, neither of us had any appetite. Sleep was made almost impossible because of the altitude, cold, excitement, and fear of what awaited us in the morning.

In the middle of the night, I struggled through the small opening of our tent. I emerged, disoriented, into the cold, black night. I stumbled and almost fell over the edge of the cliff where our campsite was perched. I was awestruck at what I saw. Mexico City stretched out below me towards the horizon. The sky was like a vast swatch of black cloth with stars punched out of it, allowing light to stream through as from some brilliant source of energy. I saw a shooting star; then another and another. I looked around at the charcoal silhouettes of Ixta's various peaks and rock formations. I stood alone, feeling very small and insignificant against the enormousness of the mountains, nature, and the universe. Finally, the cold forced me back into the tent, where I lay awake a few more hours.

Shortly after 5 a.m., Scott began to stir. He had explained that summit bids were always best started well before sunrise. Once we reached the summit, we would need plenty of daylight to descend and a large margin of safety for the unexpected. There was no need for food before our climb, as we still had no appetite. Our knapsacks were already packed, and we had slept in the clothes we were going to wear that day.

By 5:30, we were ready to go. It is the most unnerving feeling to climb a mountain in the dark. We had lights attached to headbands, so that we could keep our hands available for the treachery of the rocks. We stepped very carefully, making slow progress. As the sun began to rise, the dark shadows disappeared and the most beautiful and at the same time frightening vistas began to be revealed. Actually, I was less terrified climbing when it was dark, because I could not see how steep and challenging the terrain had become and how far below my fall would end if I lost my footing. Lack of sleep, difficulties breathing, lower blood sugar, and the drain of my emotions were making me skeptical of my chances of making it to the top.

With the slopes now steeper, I had to use my arms as well as my legs, and my muscles were aching. To make matters worse, the structure of Mt. Ixta is such that, as you reach the top of one peak the size of a large skyscraper, you are confronted, a short distance away, by yet another skyscraper to climb. I became disillusioned after my hope that we had reached the summit was dashed at the top of each peak. The altitude was robbing me of my ability to think. I became completely dependent on the words of encouragement now being frequently administered by Scott, Collin, Alex, and Murdo.

Perhaps more frightening than the climb itself was the growing anxiety, with each piece of height attained, that I could not possibly descend what I had just climbed. Finally, however, I stopped caring. I became focused only on getting to the top. It no longer mattered if I could get back down again. Scott guided us towards a geodesic silver metal hut near the summit. We stopped at the hut to rest and eat what we could. From there, the summit was only about half an hour away.

The day was spectacular. It was warm and very sunny. There was no need for any snow- or ice climbing equipment, as, except for the glacier we would traverse over flat terrain, the ground was dry. We were alternately amused and concerned, therefore, when we saw a climbing expedition from the southern United States leave the hut for the summit, roped together and wearing their crampons for gripping the snow and ice, gingerly skidding over exposed rocks. They must have been determined to use the equipment they had schlepped with them up the mountain, or maybe they had a death wish.

The time came for us to continue. At that point, I could have been more easily convinced to start down the mountain than continue to the top. Alex asked me if I was all right to go on. In a voice that surprised me by how weak it was, I answered, "I have to."

Finally, we scaled the last skyscraper. My legs and arms moved without any direction from my brain. Twenty feet from the top, I was overcome with emotion. My limbs stopped working, and I hung on a rock crying. I was as empty as when I walked away from Stacey's grave for the first time. I felt Frank behind me and then beside me. "You can do it, Ned," he repeated several times.

Getting up those last twenty feet, over the last ridge, and onto the top of Mt. Ixta could only have been courtesy of will power and adrenaline.

Once at the top, I was again overcome with emotion. But, as everyone else, one by one, appeared from behind me over the top ridge, I began to calm down and look around. The day was unusually clear, and I could see for miles and miles. I saw what Stacey wanted to see. I saw what she would have loved to see. I saw what I wished she had seen. I knew I was closer to heaven, and I touched the sky with my hands.

Scott had scrambled ahead of us to tape our successful summit bid. He captured every heart-wrenching moment and every beautiful word spoken in Stacey's memory and honor.

The ancient Hebrews were called to pray by the blowing of the shofar, a ram's horn. I began the service by blowing Stacey's lifeguard whistle. Frank and I read passages from the Yiskor service, which is the service in remembrance of the dead that is performed four times a year. With only slight modification, Frank read from that service:

In the rising of the sun and in its going down,
    we remember Stacey.
In the blowing of the wind and in the chill of
    winter, we remember Stacey.
In the opening of buds and in the rebirth of
    spring, we remember Stacey.
In the blueness of the sky and in the warmth of
    summer, we remember Stacey.
In the rustling of leaves and in the beauty of
    autumn, we remember Stacey.
In the beginning of the year and when it ends,
    we remember Stacey.
When we are weary and in need of strength, we
    remember Stacey.
When we are lost and sick at heart, we remem-
    ber Stacey.
When we have joys we yearn to share, we
    remember Stacey.
So long as we live, she too shall live, for she is
    now a part of us, as we remember Stacey.

One by one, each member of our expedition read one of Stacey's poems. Collin chose "Wind and Web," which included the words:

> The breeze is constant
> but when it becomes wind,
> everyone listens.
> The wind carries warnings and moves
> clouds.
> What we feel, is the tickle of spirits,
> nature's spirits, soothing our
> pain of captivated life.

I said the last prayer, the Kaddish, the principal Jewish prayer of mourning. Then we fastened the laminated picture of Stacey to a rock. Finally, I released the petals from the eighteen roses to the wind.

After the service, Frank and I were exhausted physically, emotionally, and spiritually. We leaned against each other and drank in the beautiful vistas that surrounded us on all sides. Nothing else was said for a very long time and I drifted into a dream-like state of peace and tranquility.

Scott had reached the summit of Mt. Ixta, and the summits of dozens of other mountains, many times before. He would later say that each summit brought with it strong emotions, but he had never experienced the power and intensity of this one.

Always conscious of safety, however, he broke into my reverie: "Ned, we have to start our descent."

The fear of how I was going to get back down returned. My fear was justified. I later learned that more injuries occur while climbing down than climbing up a mountain. At one point Frank's knees gave out, and Collin and Murdo quickly split up the contents of his knapsack between them and took his arms when necessary to ease the weight on his legs.

There are, however, good things about descending such a mountain. For one, you gain energy quickly as you leave the thinner, oxygen-deprived air of the higher altitudes. And the frightening scree slopes can be navigated on the way with the diagonal, criss-cross motion of downhill skiing. Feeling stronger and happier, I whooped with delight as I whooshed my way to the bottom of a particularly long slope. Once we reached our high camp, we broke down the tents and packed away the last of our gear. When we reached the second pass, I scrambled to the blue box and opened it. Murdo, who had some facility with Spanish, read to me several more notes left in the notepad. One said:

> Dear Stacey,
> Even though you never reached the peak of Ixta, you will belong here forever, and your presence will be felt by every climber who reaches this summit.

As we approached La Joya from the last ridge, I could see below us Miguel and Isadora and a crowd of climbers and campers all waving and shouting congratulations to us. When we finally arrived at La Joya, we were greeted like a triumphant sports team. Everyone was shouting and everyone hugged us. I was told that everyone on the mountain that day was hoping and praying for us that we would make it to the summit.

Miguel had been watching us from La Joya with his binoculars and reporting our progress to the assembled audience.

We made arrangements to have a celebration dinner at the best restaurant in Amecameca and invited Miguel and Isadora to join us. We packed Collin's van and Miguel offered to take Frank and me. I eased my aching body into the front passenger seat. Isadora, sitting in the back seat, slipped a note into my hand, which I read as we navigated the rocky road out of La Joya:

Ned,
Thanks a lot for all of your words. You teach me in the way of life, because since you appear in my father's life, he understands better the relationship between father and daughter. It can be close and hard because I am a part of him. So when you go back to Canada please be more happy because you complete a promise.

It's amazing to meet people who have a great emotional life. The tape that you gave me talks a lot of the personality of Stacey because all the groups are representing social problems, so I think she was very interested in everything that happens around her.

Just remember that in this mountain you could be in Stacey's presence. Of course she is inside your body and mind.

Many times I think of suicide, but since this experience, I can breathe again. Finally, I wish to you the best of life.
Isadora

As we traveled on a little farther, I asked Miguel if there were any better hotels in the town than the rat-free one we stayed in at the beginning. He said there was and escorted us to a motel that was acceptable by North American standards and absolutely posh by the standards we were now used to. I rented rooms for everyone at about the price of one hotel room in Toronto. We all had hot showers with clean towels.

We had our meal at a wonderful restaurant owned by a friend of Miguel's, digging into vast plates of chicken, beef, rice, and vegetables. At the end, after a dessert of tapioca pudding, we toasted Stacey, our success, life, and much, much more. That night I had the best sleep I had had in ages.

Frank and I returned to Mexico City the next day. I got a room at the airport hotel so he and I could rest until our flights. Frank's flight to Florida left in the afternoon. Mine, to Toronto, was the red-eye, leaving at midnight. After saying goodbye to Frank, I got a massage for my aching muscles, rested, and then went to dinner by myself.

I enjoyed the solitude this time. I bought a couple of English-language papers to read over dinner, to find out what had happened in the world since I stepped off it a week before. At the hotel's main restaurant, a steak house, I ordered the biggest steak on the menu, enough side dishes for three people, and to top it all off, a big piece of chocolate cake. I have no idea how much weight I lost on the mountain, but I am sure I put most of it back on at that meal.

Back in my room, it took some maneuvering to attach all of my camping gear one way or the other to my body, and grab my bags. One of the bellboys offered to assist me as I went to the counter to check out. "No, thanks," I said. "I am a mountain climber!" I am not sure what the word "schmuck" is in Spanish, but I'm sure that's what he must have said under his breath.

Before I left Amecameca, Miguel had offered to watch over the box. I left him with a few copies of Stacey's book, expecting fully that the books would disappear in fairly rapid order as people climbed Mt. Ixta and discovered what I had done. One climber predicted that the blue box would probably be a medicine cabinet in someone's bathroom within a couple of weeks. All of this mattered not a bit to me. I had accomplished what I wanted. If the box, with Stacey's book in it, remained on Mt. Ixta for one day, one week, or one month, it would not bother me for a moment. What had already come to me from the journey up Mt. Ixta and the act of leaving such a memorial to Stacey on it was beyond anything I could have possibly imagined.

I arrived in Toronto early the next morning. I had left Mexico City feeling much better than I had since Stacey died. However, as the cab approached my street, I could feel myself sinking. By the time I arrived at the house, my eyes were already beginning to tear. As I walked through the door, I fell to the floor and wept. This time, however, it was a different quality of weeping. I could not explain what had changed; I just knew that I was different than when I had left for Mexico.

CHAPTER EIGHT

back to the sleeping woman

… when blackness turns to grey,
the curtain then will fall.
After many times, I then will say,
I have been there,
I shall return one day.
FROM "STRING OF LIFE," STACEY LEVITT, 1990

IT WAS GOOD THAT I ARRIVED HOME FROM MEXICO AT THE
start of a weekend. I needed the time, before work began
on Monday, to catch up on my sleep and decompress from
the physical and emotional intensity of the trip. It also gave
me time to talk to my friends and family about the trip,
before having to occupy myself with the routine tasks
ahead of me at the office.

Everything about my house seemed unusually comfortable and luxurious. My bed felt like a cloud and familiar food

was a delight. Throughout the weekend, I maintained that extra energy that is the gift received from enduring the agonies of high altitude. I felt strong and renewed. I walked into Stacey's room and placed on her desk the stones I had brought back from the summit. I felt different in her room this time. I was still sad, but I was also proud and satisfied. It was the feeling I had when Stacey and I returned from one of our scuba adventures. I felt the joy that came from stretching our limits, together. I knew that what I had done was the right thing to do for someone as special as Stacey. Her unfinished business had been finished, and a little of her was left behind on the mountain.

Now there was another mountain for me to climb: the stack of work waiting for me at my office. But once the critical pieces were attended to, I turned my attention to the digital tapes of Scott's recording of our climb. As with almost everything about my life since Stacey died, there was a story of human kindness and compassion in connection with the camera we took with us up the mountain. At the time, digital video cameras had not entered the retail market in any significant way. They were still very expensive and were mostly used by professionals. Prior to our expedition, I had been working with a producer, Rob Engman, in making a pilot for a television program about franchising. In the process I had told him about Stacey and my intended climb of Mt. Ixta. I did not realize that Rob possessed the heart and soul of a poet. He entrusted me with a very expensive, state-of-the-art digital video camera, at no charge, for the climb. The lightness of the camera and the power of its new technology helped us capture some amazing moments and images on tape. Now I had to decide what to do with the raw footage. We had recorded far more than we needed. Some scenes were extraordinary and some were quite ordinary.

Rob's generosity was unending. Not only did he make one of his high-tech Avid machines and editing suites available to me, but he also assigned one of his editors to the task. The editor and I prepared the tapes over several weeks. It was fascinating to work with such technological wizardry. You can capture a single image, syllable, or note in a song and "drop" it seamlessly into another scene. I asked Marni to record some of her songs so we could use them in the background of the tape. While the end product was not of professional quality, it was very powerful and moving.

I slipped back into my routine of trying to regain what I had lost. Now the focus was not exclusively Stacey. I had to deal with all the other things that are swept along with you in the wake of the death of a loved one. I had lost ambition, confidence, a feeling of security, and the will and ability to concentrate on business. Even though clients respected me and cared about me, they still had needs that had to be met. My practice had to be regenerated. I gradually became more capable of doing legal work, but, as the senior member of the firm, my main job was to attract new clients and business for the firm. The emptiness inside me made that a much more difficult task.

I was making small gains, week by week, but I often found myself drifting back to thoughts about Mt. Ixta and wondering what was happening to the box and its contents. After a couple of months, I had to call Miguel to connect with him and find out what was transpiring on the mountain.

"You won't believe what is happening!" Miguel told me. "People have been so moved by what you did and Stacey's poetry. Many people have already left messages in the notebook and some come to pray at the box."

"What?"

"Yes, they have named it Stacey's Caja Azul, Stacey's Blue Box, and it has become a meeting place for climbers."

"Miguel, I am not prepared for this. This scares me a bit."

"No, it's a good thing, Ned. Many people write about how Stacey's spirit gives them courage and how beautiful she was and how beautiful her words are. This is a very good thing."

"Have you had to replace many books?"

"Not one! Everyone respects the book and leaves it for others, just like you said on the sign. The mountaineering club members all love it and watch over things when they climb. I have given the book to some people who very much wanted a copy. Can you send more to me?"

"Yes, Miguel, I will send some more soon."

Then the letters started to arrive, many of them asking for a copy of Stacey's book. Sometimes I would receive a couple on the same day and then nothing for weeks. The unpredictability intensified the suspense and my desire to receive them. Letters arrived from Mexico, the U.S., France, Switzerland, the Czech Republic, and Israel. Mt. Ixta is a very popular mountain to climb and, while Mexicans and Americans are the most frequent visitors, people from all over the world climb there.

These letters expressed so many wonderful sentiments — and sometimes the writer's own pain in losing a loved one. I read about their triumphs, too, and their dreams. I came to realize that people who attempt to climb, no matter whether to the summit or not, are already a self-selected group. They are people who are searching for something: exhilaration, adrenaline, beauty, solitude, solace, spiritualism. They are open to experiences and wanting to be affected, if not moved. These people have to overcome the physical challenges of altitude and climbing steep terrain just to arrive at the second pass, where they must decide whether to stop and be contented with their accomplishments or to face the awesome challenges of the difficult climb ahead. At this point they discover, or are confronted by, Stacey's Caja Azul and the power of her poetry.

There are many memorials on the mountain, but none that tell so complete a story; none that reveal who the deceased was, and certainly none that reveal the thoughts and character of the deceased in their own words. No other memorials there invite the climber to "communicate" with the deceased and their loved ones. It astonished me how many people, in their letters and entries in the notebooks, wrote to Stacey in the first person. Others wrote to God, to their deceased loved ones, or to our family.

I could not know all of the thoughts of those who climbed to the box and read Stacey's poetry, but I could see that the memorial was taking on a life of its own. Sometimes I would receive a letter that expressed concern that the book was missing from the box. In one of my telephone calls to Miguel to tell him about some of the letters I had received, I mentioned the problem.

"Ned, I have investigated this, because the book is still there," he said. "Apparently, some people take Stacey's book with them to the summit, but they always return it to the box on the way down. The climbers that follow directly after them find the box empty."

I replied to each letter, enclosing a copy of Stacey's book. I called Miguel from time to time with reports on what I was receiving and to find out what he was observing.

"Ned, I will send you the original notebook and the one I replaced it with," Miguel said. "They are both full. I put a third one in the box. You will not believe what people have been writing."

"Thank you so much, Miguel, you are wonderful to take care of the box for me."

"No problem, it is not only my pleasure, but it is a privilege. It also helps me right now because my wife, Mina, is very sick with cancer."

"Oh, Miguel, I am so sorry. What do the doctors say?"

"They hope for the best, but they are not optimistic."

"I will pray for her, Miguel."

"Thank you my friend."

When the first notebooks arrived from Miguel, I felt like I was a boy again on that birthday when I came home from school to find a shiny new bicycle waiting for me in the driveway. I opened the courier pouch slowly, worrying that I might damage these now sacred texts. I looked at each of the more than two hundred entries in the notebooks. I tried to decipher as much as I could of the ones written in Spanish, even though I cannot read or speak Spanish. When I came to one written in English, I read it several times. I felt as if I was there at the box with the writer. I phoned Frank and told him I would get a photocopy of the notebooks to him right away.

My next passion was to get the entries in Spanish translated into English. Fortunately, one of Marni's friends, Danna, had been learning Spanish and was dating a young man from Mexico. The two of them made the perfect team to do the translations. I could hardly contain myself while the translations were being done. The wait was well worth it. A few examples can be found on the next couple of pages:

As a young climber, and a woman, and a runner, my heart could not go out to you more. I will think of Stacey as I climb mountains and run and do all the things she might have done, and I'll whisper her name to the winds when I reach summits, and maybe she will hear me — saludos y fuerza.
With much feeling to all the family,
Alexandra Baer

Dear Stacey,
It's a strong feeling to meet you here. Yes, you are a beautiful rose, I saw this in your picture. I believe your soul is still here. Thanks for letting me meet you.
dis, Denmark

In this solitary nook of the world, a little closer to heaven, nature demands with respect and imposes greatness; the smallest pebble and the lightest flutter of wind add to this incomprehensible beauty, and every moment of light and shade saturates the skin's pores, and you can almost hear God.
Ulises Zamora M., Mexico City

May your mother take you in her soul,
your friends in their hearts
and God in the palm of his hand.
Hector Mendoza

Stacey,

My name is Ricardo Tabique and I've come to say thanks to God for saving my wife, Gaby, and keeping her in good health, and also to ask him to take care of my baby, Dianita (may she rest in peace). Today is my first time coming here and I really feel close to God, and since you, Stacey, are with Him, I ask you too to care for my little baby. Thank you.

Hi Stacey,

This place is incredible. I know you're with God. You have a huge family.
God treats people like he does roses: He cuts them at their best moment, and only He knows when that is.

Hi Stacey,

My name is Elisa, this is my first time here. I'm twelve years old and my dad brought me here. Even though I didn't want to come at first, I liked it a lot because I exercised and had fun. I hope that now you're with God.

Reading Stacey's words, I feel alive. I can feel the mountain air caressing my face, I can feel the roughness of the rocks on my hands, I feel the rays of sun warming my body, and I hear the clouds saying that we have to carry on, live life to its fullest. In short, a wonder of God.
Aziel Ruiz Juarez

Through Bereaved Families of Ontario, I began showing the video of my climb up Mt. Ixta to other bereaved parents. After one showing, Margaret McGovern, at the time the executive director, told me that there were a lot of powerful and helpful messages in my story and that I might want to do something more with it. Later she introduced me to Karen Shopsowitz, an up-and-coming documentary maker who had directed a sensitive and insightful television program, *A Mother's Grief.*

My initial meeting with Karen was, as they say, "love at first sight." She was remarkably easy to talk to (a good quality in a documentary filmmaker) and immediately grasped everything I said. I deluged her with information and stories about Stacey, her book, my suffering, and the climb, but she never appeared to be bored or overwhelmed. When our talk came to a close, she said she was interested in making a TV documentary. There was only one problem. Karen's mother was dying from cancer, and Karen needed to invest a lot of time and energy helping her. I understood in a way that would have eluded me in my former life. We agreed to meet again when she was able and to move the project forward slowly, taking advantage of any spare time she might have available.

As November 1997, the first anniversary of my climb up Mt. Ixta, approached, I felt drawn to return there. I wanted to recapture some of the magic of the first climb, and I also wanted to experience firsthand the effect Stacey's memorial was having on people. My decision was made one night in early October in a telephone conversation with Miguel.

"Would you be able, Miguel, to climb with me if I came there by the second week of November?" I knew his wife was very sick.

"I have discussed this with Mina. She has insisted that I climb Mt. Ixta with you. She knows how much it would mean to me. I think she will be okay without me for a couple of days."

I mentioned this to Karen. "Ned, I would really like to get some footage of this trip. My husband, Mark, is a cameraman and I would love for him to accompany you." The deal was struck, and I made plans to return to the Sleeping Woman.

I wanted to meet some of the people who had corresponded with me. With Miguel and Isadora's help, it was arranged that Terre Hernandez, Tobin Marsh, and Jorge and Carlos Ortiz Guzman, all experienced climbers, would be part of the expedition. I was told that they not only accepted the invitation but were ecstatic about meeting me. I was shocked, however, when Mark and I entered the terminal in Mexico City, and they were all there waving to us, huge smiles on their faces. Terre was waving a copy of Stacey's book, which I had sent to her. Jorge told me that many climbers "know Stacey" and are moved by the memorial. When I saw Isadora, we embraced with such warmth and affection I could not contain my tears. With lots of hugs and some tears all around, the feeling was family right away.

The next day we all met at the hotel for a leisurely breakfast and lots of time for conversation. Then we were off to the mountain.

We set up camp at La Joya, just like the first time. Once we were settled we did a warmup climb to the first pass. I had decided that, on this trip, I would only go as high as the second pass and the box. Frank could not get away, and Miguel was the leader of the expedition. I was amazed that I felt so good and was experiencing minimal side effects from the altitude. I have been told that blood cells have memory and that subsequent trips to high altitude are easier. Unfortunately, Mark was feeling the effects very badly and had difficulty eating and sleeping.

In the morning, many climbers stopped by our campsite to meet me and tell me how much Stacey meant to them. Mark interviewed Terre, while I watched, about her ordeal of being robbed just before she climbed to the second pass and saw Stacey's memorial. She speaks only Spanish, but Miguel translated for me and I could see how emotional it was for her to tell the story. She could hardly speak for her sobbing.

Later, when we stopped for a rest at the first pass, Carlos and I attempted to communicate in French, the only language with which we both shared some facility. He had tears in his eyes when he told me how much Stacey meant to him and how much it meant to him that I was climbing with him. While we sat there talking, a stream of runners went by. They were in a mountain marathon race that takes place there every year. It attracts racers from all over the world and receives a lot of television coverage in Europe. The Sky TV helicopter hovering above added to the feeling of drama. I could not believe the speed at which the marathoners ran, when I was lucky in these altitudes just to walk at half my normal pace. I thought it fitting that they would be going past the memorial to Stacey, who had died while running. The winner ran from the base of the mountain to the summit and back in three and a half hours. It took me five days the first time. One unfortunate runner came by covered in blood. He had stumbled on the way down and fallen, but adrenaline and will had kept him going.

Midway from the first pass to the second, I encountered a man who I knew was on the mountain and was looking for me. He was climbing down from the second pass with his two teenage sons. He was some distance away when he spotted us. He knew right away that it was me, because he recognized Miguel and Isadora. He moved with the speed and dexterity of someone very familiar with the mountain, closing the distance between us in amazing time. In broken English, he said again and again how much he loved Stacey and how much everyone who climbed there loved her. I gave him a copy of her book, and he kissed it.

Many people joined us at the memorial, as Miguel had posted signs for several weeks that we were coming to celebrate its first anniversary. I retrieved the now very tattered and written on first book and replaced it with a fresh one. I removed the current full notebook and substituted a new blank one. I had brought along a couple of bottles of wine, and we toasted Stacey and life.

We were not as lucky with the weather this time, as it was very foggy, with lots of drizzle. This did not, however, dampen the party atmosphere that quickly developed. I had a chance to meet everyone who gathered there and, either in English, broken English, or through translation, learn about them, what the mountain meant to them, and the feelings they had about Stacey. I looked longingly up the mountain and had a small pang of regret that I was not going higher this time.

Mark was really feeling sick, so, with many warm embraces and back slaps, I said goodbye to those who remained at the pass and our group headed back to La Joya. As we descended, I realized how familiar the mountain had become to me. I was confident and comfortable now.

Miguel invited Mark and me for dinner at his house in Mexico City and to clean up before our flight back to Toronto. He lived with his wife, Mina, his two daughters, Isadora and Erica, and his mother and her husband. The house was charming, situated on a quiet street in a middle-class neighborhood. The tranquility and calm of the street were belied by the presence of iron gates at the end of each driveway, there to prevent the ever-present threat of auto theft.

Mina was not well enough to eat with us and, in fact, did not feel up to meeting me. I said I understood and asked them to give her a small gold cross on a chain that I had brought as a gift. It was a strange feeling to share a wonderful meal with Miguel and his family, while Mina lay a short distance from us dying. By then, however, I had become used to the strange, unexpected, and unusual.

CHAPTER NINE

a beginning

Helpless and lonely,
plunging deeper into the dark,
unknown depths below.
A shimmer of light,
small and faint.
Hope,
an ending,
a beginning.
FROM "LOST," STACEY LEVITT, 1990

ONE WEEK AFTER RETURNING FROM MEXICO I RECEIVED A letter from Miguel:

November 24, 1997

Dear Friend,
I am writing you this after all the suffering journey of my wife has finished. Now she is resting and I'm sure, also very happy. Yesterday we buried her, the day before yesterday she passed away. Today she is in heaven.

I can't tell you that she didn't suffer, she did, but never accordingly with the doctor's expectations and similar illness patients' stories told me by their relatives. As a matter of fact she had very short agony and she died without any pain medicine. So I feel that the grace of God was very merciful to her.

In these past two weeks, I was very close to her, attending all her needs, talking a lot, playing the keyboard for her, giving her medicine, being aware how she had moments of grace promoted by our praying and her faith, suffering with her pain and rejoicing with her good moments.

We did not want to accept the possibility to extend her life for perhaps one or two days because it meant to put her in a cold hospital bed and make wounds and scars in her body, which she did not accept in the past, so finally we let her go, as she would like it.

I have many other things to tell you, but I cannot write them now, because it hurts a lot. I'll do it in the near future. In the meantime, receive my best wishes for your family and also let me give you regards from all my family and from Carlos, Jorge and Terre, who were with me in these past two days.
Your friend,
Miguel

Miguel and I were now joined as brothers in grief; a grief known only to those who have loved deeply and lost far, far too soon. I read his letter several times and the last sentence many times. I was stunned by the fact that Carlos, Jorge, and Terre, previously complete strangers, had been united through Stacey to bring to Miguel the comfort and support I wanted so much to provide but could not.

In the months that followed the second climb, Karen worked sporadically on the documentary. We would talk from time to time about her mother and what she was going through. Her mother suffered, and so did Karen, but through it all Karen kept showing me her extraordinary personality: she was warm, vibrant, inquisitive (another good quality in a documentary maker), and optimistic. She was engaged in an ancient ritual of caring for a dying parent. However, like Miguel and me, Karen finally had to experience that horrible tearing of the heart and soul that comes, yet again, from a loss out of time.

I attended Karen's mother's funeral and returned that night to the Shiva house for evening prayers. I spent more time there than normal for me, and Karen seemed to want to talk to me. Our conversation ranged over many things, and then she said, matter-of-factly, "Ned, I am ready now to finish the documentary." I humored her — I certainly did not expect her to have the energy or will to complete such a challenging project for quite a while.

Well, I just did not know Karen. Within days of the end of Shiva, she was in motion. Before I knew it, plans were made to return to Mt. Ixta on October 14, 1999, with Mark as the cameraman, a soundman, Miguel as cook and guide, and Isadora as production assistant. On this trip, production scheduling would prevent us from climbing higher than the second pass and Stacey's Caja Azul. In Mexico, two young male friends of Isadora's would be hired for schlepping equipment and a freelance photographer from Mexico City would be retained to take still pictures on the climb.

As far as I was concerned, the most important person of all on the expedition would be Karen. I said, "Karen, you are not going to try and climb, are you?" She answered in a tone of voice that would have cowed the toughest mountain climber, "Try and stop me!"

And so it was back to Mt. Ixta with a new entourage. The challenges of climbing were still present, but I was now seasoned and felt very comfortable knowing what was coming. Mark and the soundman had additional challenges, as they had to carry heavy equipment. The soundman, a young guy, fell into the altitude trap awaiting the inexperienced climber. He felt good and moved at a tremendously fast pace at times on our climb to the box, but he paid for this, big time, that night. He became ill, with severe headaches, chills, and vomiting. Fortunately there were enough experienced people around to nurse him back to health. I could not believe how Karen was keeping pace, even as she directed shots and interviewed me and the people who kept moving in and out of our expedition.

Mt. Ixta is huge, but the reactions I kept getting from people who sought me out to meet me and talk with me made me see that the mountain was a small community. One couple said that the wife was inspired by Stacey and started climbing higher, to the delight of her husband. I met a man leading a group of high school students who spoke so warmly to me and embraced me. But the most astounding expressions of emotion were yet to be revealed to me. Miguel had said, as we started to climb, "A few things have been put in the box that I can't believe or fully understand. However, I don't want to tell you what they are. I simply want you to be prepared that you will see some unusual things."

Arriving at the box was much more pleasure than pain, compared with the first two climbs. I was looking forward to gathering up another notebook full of wonderful messages. This time, the making of the documentary was paramount. Nonetheless, neither I nor any of the members of our group, except Miguel and Isadora, were prepared for what I found when I opened the lid of the box. Along with some drawings and colorful stones, a small red Bible and a metal container, the size of a large matchbox, had been left in the box. I examined the metal container and noticed that there was an inscription on the side: a woman's name and the dates of her birth and death. She had died seven years previously. Miguel explained that the box contained the ashes of a deceased woman. I was stunned. Maybe this whole thing was becoming more than I could be comfortable with.

I hatched a plan to find a priest in the town who might take charge of the Bible and metal container. This became a rather difficult task, as it was Sunday afternoon and the priests, having completed their Sunday morning tasks, were off on other business. Finally, we found a student priest, who said that there really was no way the church could take charge of the ashes, which then made sense to me. I had assumed that the church would readily take charge of the ashes, but, of course, these were the ashes of a deceased woman, and the church had no instructions from her heirs to deal with them. In the end, Miguel offered to take the ashes back up the mountain, at a later date, and place them somewhere central there. He would then spread the word about what he had done and hope that the person who put them in Stacey's blue box would contact him. For sure, I was not comfortable with the ashes remaining in the blue box. I did not want to encourage the creation of a shrine.

Back at the hotel in Mexico City, we all gathered for a sumptuous dinner at the same steak house I ate at after the first climb, to celebrate all the wonderful footage captured on this climb. Karen was confident she had lots to work with from the video of the first climb and the film from the second and third climbs.

As the dinner got under way, I was feeling great. There had been no episodes of crying or feelings of deep pain at all on this trip. It came as a shock to me, then, when, just after we had all ordered and I was raising my wine glass to make a toast, I had an unusual feeling start in the pit of my stomach and spread to my chest and throughout my body. At first it frightened me. As I toasted Stacey, I began to shake and cry. "None of you knew her. I wish you had, then you would understand what I have lost," I said. It was not like I heard Stacey's voice, but words just seemed to come into my head, from where I did not know. With these words, I understood for the first time what I had been doing. Why I went to Mexico. Why I established the memorial. Why I had been so eager to share Stacey's poetry with others.

I told the group what the words were. "Dad, I am sorry I had to leave. I know how much it has hurt you. But I have left you three gifts: my love, my spirit, and my poetry. If you share them with the world, people will come into your life and help heal your broken heart."

Karen's documentary, *I Am a Rose: A Father's Journey*, was a work of art. The background music and only song used, "I Am," was written and sung by Marni. The impact of Stacey's poetry was never more forceful than when it was read by voice-over actors, who lent a dramatic interpretation to the words. However, perhaps the most important ingredients to the impact of the documentary were the gifts of exceptional insight, creativity, and sensitivity that grief had bestowed on Karen during its production. The documentary was jointly funded by the CBC and Vision Television and was broadcast many times.

In anticipation of viewers wanting to have more information and a copy of Stacey's poetry book, a friend of mine put up a beautiful website for me, www.iamarose.com. In a flash of creativity, someone suggested that we add a "virtual blue box" to function on the site like the box on Mt. Ixta, allowing visitors to make entries and read the entries of others. And once again, now in this new medium, I was given the opportunity to connect with people and hear, firsthand, how Stacey and her poetry had moved them. The website also lets people communicate privately with us by e-mail. So, in addition to the many entries in the virtual blue box, I have received many, many e-mails after each airing of the documentary.

In his book *Ghost Rider*, rock drummer Neil Peart says that after the death of his daughter (coincidentally a friend of Stacey's from school) and then his wife a year later, "There would be no peace for me, no *life* for me, until I learned to forgive life for what it had done to me, forgive others for still being alive, and eventually forgive *myself* for being alive."

It had been a constant struggle over the years that followed Stacey's death for me to grant such forgiveness. As I did, I found that, as Leonard Fein, a bereaved father, said in his book, *Against the Dying of the Light*, I began to live with the loss, not in the loss. I would move forward and then seem to fall back. This was unnerving and sometimes frightening.

I came to realize, however, that the pattern of grief is that of a spiral. While it looks and feels like you are circling back to the same painful places, in fact you do return to do more grief work, but each time from a higher elevation. I wanted to be treated like everyone else, but at the same time I wanted to be treated differently. I remember the first time I laughed, some eight or nine months after Stacey's death, and how strange it felt. From the time Stacey died, my life was changed and every experience thereafter was measured, framed, colored, altered, diminished, or heightened by that fact. In some things, this helped, while other things were made more difficult and certainly more complex.

As my daughter Jacqueline's wedding date, November 2, 2002, approached, it was time to write my speech. I consulted some other bereaved parents who had been through this for advice. The consensus was I had to find a balance between bringing Stacey into this most important event and not letting it overshadow the joy everyone felt for Jacqueline. This was no simple task. In the end, it was best to let Stacey speak for herself. I simply read this poem, written by her in 1987, when she was ten years old:

Lovely Lady

Lovely lady, lovely lady,
Why do you hide?
Lovely lady, lovely lady,
Come be my bride.

You are passionate and gentle.
You fill me with pride.
Lovely lady, lovely lady,
Come be my bride.

Your voice is soft and steady.
Your hair is shiny and smooth.
When you walk you glide.
Lovely, lady, lovely lady,
come be my bride.

I will climb the highest mountain.
I will dance on a star.
I will never leave your side, if
You'll only be my bride.

Lovely, lady, lovely lady,
you're as sweet as honey.
You're as beautiful as the shining sea.
You're as delicate as a dove.
Oh! Lovely lady, lovely lady,
Won't you share your love?

Lovely lady, lovely lady,
The sea you shall have.
The sun you shall cherish.
The wind you shall ride.
Lovely lady, lovely lady,
Won't you be my bride?

What I could not have known when I chose to read that poem at Jacqueline's wedding was that Stacey and the poem would, yet again, take me on another voyage of discovery.

On April 14, 2003, I received a letter from San Antonio, Texas.

Dear Cheryl, Ned and Levitt Family,
There is a young man (now 30) who went to camp with Stacey. His name is Marc Reeves, son of Elaine and Rob Reeves, formerly of Toronto. Marc proposed to our daughter, Dorian, on the moonlit beach in Kauai, Hawaii, this past February. He read her "Lovely Lady," and at the end of the poem, asked Dorian to be his bride. They are getting married November 1, 2003.

Marc and Dorian are two very special people. They love life and they love people. Marc introduced Dorian to *I Am a Rose* about a year ago. She treasures this book and often reads from it to her 2nd grade class in the San Francisco area.

Stacey continues to touch many lives. She certainly has touched ours. We hope someday to meet you, and we will continue to read Stacey's beautiful poetry.
Most sincerely,
Judy Goldstein

I told this beautiful story many times to many people, but I did not realize there was to be a sequel. Six months later, Dorian wrote to us:

Hi! My name is Dorian Goldstein, daughter of Judy Goldstein, who wrote to you about my fiancé (Marc Reeves) and my story of our connection to your beautiful daughter, Stacey.

Marc and his brother, Adam, went to camp

with Stacey for a few years. Their memory of her is of a truly outgoing friend who they had a lot of fun with!

I could only wish that I could have had the privilege to meet your daughter… Her wisdom and understanding of life's beauties, as well as her zest for each day, radiates and glows… A true angel, sent here for a purpose. You are right, as you wrote in the introduction to *I Am a Rose*: "… and when you finish reading them, you will know Stacey." How lucky we are to have this poetry each day. We have shared this, and Stacey's story, with many of our friends.

Marc is much like Stacey. His love of life, sincere warmth and kindness, and wisdom enriches the lives of those around him. That is probably why when he proposed to me on a beach in Kauai, February 19, and read "Lovely Lady," it all seemed so natural.

Our wedding is November 1st in San Antonio, Texas … Right around the corner! We are getting so very excited and plan on reading one of Stacey's poems during our ceremony. Her legacy lives on and touches so many … My mom is sending you all an invitation. We would absolutely LOVE IT if you could come celebrate this happy time with us! We all really would like to meet you!

Stacey and your loving family have touched our lives.

Fondly,
Dorian Goldstein

When I finished reading this note from Dorian, I gave it to Cheryl. "What do you think, Cheryl? Do you want to go?"

"Let's do it," she responded, without hesitation.

The Goldsteins and the Reeves were delighted that we agreed to attend the wedding. In the exchanges that followed, I began to get a picture of a very special group of people. I sensed that while this turn of events was unusual for them, it was not totally out of character. I was even asked if I would say a few words at the wedding. On the plane to San Antonio, I scribbled a few notes for my short speech. My thought was I would mostly explain why we were there and wish the couple well in their marriage.

Both Cheryl and I wondered what this adventure would be like. We were nervous about it. We are not shy people, but we were both very aware of the fact that we were complete strangers attending a very intimate event in the life of a family. We added a few days to the trip; if the wedding experience was mediocre, we could at least have a pleasant vacation in a place we had never visited before.

From the moment we entered the hospitality suite in the hotel where we and other out-of-town wedding guests were staying, we felt like old friends, if not family. Just change the accents and these people could have been our friends in Toronto. Many guests came from out of town, so, as the weekend events unfolded, it was not unusual, after the exchange of names, to enter this kind of dialogue:

"What connects you to the wedding? Are you with the bride's side?"

"No."

"Oh, are you friends or family of the groom's side?"

"Neither."

"Then why are you here?"

"My wife, Cheryl, and I are internationally renowned wedding crashers and this is the hundredth wedding we have crashed."

"Ha, Ha! No, seriously, *why are you here?*"

I thought we should not tell the story before the wedding, feeling that Dorian and Marc might want the story and the reading of Stacey's poem to be a surprise. This was not to be, as I soon realized that a number of people already knew why we were there. As I began to tell the truth to those who posed the right questions, they either already knew the story and were happy to meet us, or they listened to the story for the first time, with tears in their eyes.

The more we participated in the weekend of events around the wedding, the more we felt like we were attending a wedding of long-standing friends. The vacation activities paled compared with the wedding events, and Cheryl and I kept asking ourselves how we could explain to our family and friends back home what we were living through that weekend and the feelings we were experiencing.

What I did figure out, as I got to know Dorian better, personally and through others, was that she shared many of Stacey's qualities and characteristics, which explained, in part, why she connected so intensely with her poetry.

As we sat in the sanctuary waiting for the bridal party to walk down the aisle, it felt like so many other weddings of friends' children we have attended. That is how deeply we had bonded with the families. Then my thoughts turned to why we were there, and I said to Cheryl, as a warning to prepare herself emotionally, "Cheryl, remember why we are here. In a moment we are going to hear Stacey's poem read during a wedding ceremony of complete strangers." Cheryl's expression changed, as she pondered what I had just said, then she nodded her concurrence.

What followed was as wonderful, as beautiful, as emotional as anything that had taken place since Stacey died. The rabbi told the story of Stacey's tragic death, the connection to Marc, the publishing of her poetry book, the use of the poem by Marc to ask Dorian to marry him, the couple's generous invitation to us to attend the wedding, and our courage to accept. Then, after observing that Stacey wrote the poem at the age of ten, he read it with such power and such meaning that there was not a dry eye in the house. Then all three hundred people in attendance turned to us, as Cheryl could no longer contain her emotions and broke down weeping.

Strangely, the shedding of tears did not detract from the wedding but took everything to a higher, more joyful level, beyond anything anyone in attendance had ever experienced. Many, many people, now knowing who we were and why we were there, confirmed as much throughout the reception that night and into the next day's farewell brunch.

One morning, seven years after my first trip up Mt. Ixta, I phoned Miguel. After a few moments, I said, "Miguel, it's been seven years now since I put the box on Mt. Ixta and you have been so wonderful to look after it for me. But I was wondering if you have had enough. I could come down and respectfully take it off the mountain and put a plaque up."

"No, no. I am happy to continue. It means a lot to me. I am honoured to be the official keeper of Stacey's Caja Azul."

I thanked him. "You are a good man, Miguel. You have been very kind to me and my family."

The box remains on the Sleeping Woman to this day.

Climbers continue to make entries in the notebooks and to send me letters. Memorials are important in helping those left behind to carry on. Memorials are for remembering, but they should also inspire and teach. A good memorial tells the world that the person lived, was loved, and still matters in this world. I have created other memorials to Stacey, but I have come to the conclusion that the most meaningful and important memorial to her is how I live my life. By helping other bereaved parents through their ordeal, an increasingly busy part of my life, and by sharing her poetry, I continue Stacey's influence on the world. I have learned that bereaved parents fear losing their children a second time when no one thinks about them, mentions their name, or feels their influence anymore. I, too, have been fighting against Stacey's second death.

I have also learned that grief is like a searing wall of pain that one cannot get around, over, or under. Even though, at first, you cannot even touch it, eventually you must go through it. When I found myself on the other side of the wall, I also found Stacey again. I found I could then remember the good times and bring her image and voice to my mind and hold on to the beauty of her life. No one can heal grief in another person, and time alone does not heal it. Rather, the human spirit heals itself when given an opportunity to do so. That opportunity came for me when others, strangers and friends, gave me the warmth of their presence, the strength of their understanding, and the power of their love.

I remember Stacey, after she had written a poem she liked, bouncing down the stairs to share it with everyone. I could never have imagined then what that poetry would someday come to mean to me or where it would take me. I have met hundreds of people I would never have met, engaged in hundreds of conversations I would never have had, and seen things I would never have seen or would have overlooked had Stacey not died. I have been enriched and my eyes have been opened. Would I take her back, if I could, and give back these abundant gifts? The answer could not be more obvious. But I cannot, and so, instead, I will continue as I have. I will accept her gifts, and I will say, "Thank you, Stacey."

I have a picture in my mind of Stacey, at seventeen, all by herself, on the three-day solo portion of her Outward Bound program in British Columbia. She was given little food and equipment and had to survive on her own skills and wits. As part of the requirements of the program, she had to write herself a letter containing her thoughts from the experience, which was then to be sent to her several months after she returned home. An excerpt from that letter sums up her spirit so well that we have added it to her poetry book, put it on a memorial plaque in Stacey's Garden at our synagogue, and engraved it on her headstone at the cemetery. Here's what she wrote:

> The fog rolled down the hills to get me and
> I stood strong. The rain fell from the
> clouds to chill me and I stayed warm and
> dry. The wind blew from all directions to
> rob me of my shelter but my tarp stayed. I
> conquered mountains in my path and
> looked behind me with a smile...

Loves ya, Stace!

helping and being helped

EXCEPT FOR THE COURSE I TOOK WITH BEREAVED FAMILIES of Ontario to become a group facilitator, I have no education or credentials in bereavement. Mine was on-the-job training, augmented by an insatiable appetite to read and learn about bereavement, particularly parental bereavement. I have discovered a great deal about this all too common human condition. Perhaps the fact that I am not encumbered by any school of thought, professional rules, or patients' expectations will help me offer something of value to those who must cope with loss in their lives and those who wish to help them.

Looking at loss in its broadest sense, it is safe to say that it would be almost impossible to live a life without loss and bereavement Loss is experienced from the day we are born, as we lose the warmth and security of the womb, and the experience continues as we are weaned from the breast, face intruders on our turf — they're called brothers and sisters — lose childhood friends as they move away (or we do) from our neighborhoods, lose in relationships before, during, or after marriage, lose our jobs, lose our youth, lose our health. In a very real way, who we are is defined by our losses and how we have reacted to them. The nature of the loss and its timing and severity will be major factors in how and how profoundly the loss will affect us and shape us.

Loss can affect our personalities — witness the crusader for causes, the independence of many adults who lost a parent at a young age, and the frequency with which unresolved grief is at the core of depression. One pundit wrote that he was ten per cent of what happened to him in life and ninety per cent how he reacted to what happened to him in life.

Loss and profound grief from the loss can kill you, for example through suicide or attacks on your immune system. But this kind of grief can liberate you from unhappy lifetime patterns of behavior, unleash your creativity and strength, and allow you to reach your true potential. In the early stages of my bereavement, I became aware of the incredibly empowering nature of my loss. For a long time, I no longer had any ego, any ambition, any fear of dying, any concern for what people thought of me, or any expectations of life. I was an empty vessel, except for who I really was.

Even as I was wrestling with the enormous pain, I began to see that this was a unique opportunity to grow as a person and to alter, whether slightly or profoundly, how I would be and who I would be in the future. My thoughts were never clearer and my actions never so purposeful. It showed, as I had an impact on the people I encountered on a journey I never would have even attempted before.

Regrettably, in North America we seem to live in a death-denying culture. We do not, in our schools, explore loss, its effects on us, and the ways we can deal with it. Our religious institutions, whose mandate includes dealing with death and bereavement, too often focus on the ritual rather than the human need. We too easily turn away from the bereaved — to let them be alone with their loss or, perhaps, to not become infected by that loss. Because we have so little education and experience in the language of loss, we worry that we will say the wrong thing, so we bring greater hurt upon the griever by not saying anything at all.

As a result, many people who are struggling with loss become isolated from the very human contact and support they so desperately crave and need. This is not just forced upon the bereaved, but it is facilitated by the bereaved person's complete cooperation. We quickly learn not to burden people who just can't or won't understand. We feel we are protecting our family by not sharing our feelings of loss with them. We force ourselves to hide the crippling pain from co-workers, with whom we spend the majority of our time.

If someone we know walked into a room struggling with crutches, most of us would offer them assistance, help him or her to a comfortable chair, and inquire about the injury and its causes. Compare that with most people's reactions when a bereaved parent returns to work! Having said that, I have come to realize that a small proportion of people will always help others in distress, emotional or otherwise, and a small proportion of people will never help. The vast majority of people would help if they knew how or were invited to do so.

It is as challenging to ask for help or accept it as it is to offer or provide it. Helping the bereaved is a dance between two people, each with his or her own role, expectations, and needs. The result can be disastrous or profoundly beautiful and healing.

Within a general framework and patterns of response to loss, each person reacts in his or her own way, according to personality and view of life. The following are some of the things I have observed or learned on my journey thus far. They may not be applicable to the experience of some, but they will be familiar, and perhaps make sense, to many.

Tears: As humans, we respond to the pain of loss by crying. That said, "Big boys don't cry." Men are forced to project an image of strength and courage. Tears are a sign that everything is not right and that the person is at least in a temporary state of weakness. I am forever amazed when people who are in enormous pain apologize for crying. When we cry, we tend to hide our face or leave the company of others. How unfortunate, when the very presence of others, their touch, and the sound of their voices might be exactly what we need. The common response to another's tears is, "Don't cry, everything will be all right." Nonsense. Nothing may ever be right again. Do you think a newly bereaved parent even wants everything to be all right? The strength to let the person cry in your presence, without offering solutions, perhaps offering only a hug, may be all that is needed at that moment.

Touch: In our uptight world, it is dangerous to counsel touching. However, within the bounds of good judgment, many people benefit enormously from touch and embrace when they are in pain from loss. So much is communicated by physical contact that it often renders speech unnecessary.

Acknowledgment: One of the most powerful things we can do for someone who has recently experienced loss is to acknowledge their great pain. We should not say that we understand, if it is a loss we have not experienced, but we can always confirm that we are aware that they are in pain from that loss. Whether one views that as the horribly distorted concept of "pity" or not, it matters to the one in pain.

Speaking: The most important person to be speaking in a bereavement dance is the bereaved person. The very act of talking about the pain, the deceased, the nature of the loss, is therapeutic. Being a good listener for someone who has experienced loss is very valuable — more valuable than offering advice. In fact, in many loss situations, there really is no advice that can change past events or the consequences of those events. Listening, coupled with acknowledgement of the pain, over time, can work wonders.

Honesty: Being honest about your pain gives relief and permits others to react in a way that is more useful to you. Often it is much harder to put on a brave face than to simply state that it is not a good time or a good day and why. The people around you, if they are able and willing, can then support you, alter your or their schedule or environment, or take some other action that might help you get through a rough patch. Being honest about your ability to help a person in pain is better than taking on a task you are not ready for at that moment. Too often, we view the person in pain as incapable of accepting the limits on our ability to help them.

Accepting: Accepting what has happened and its consequences is one of the most important goals for those who have experienced loss. Accepting is not the same as knowing. Knowing is in the brain; accepting is in the heart. The path from knowing to accepting is often long and winding, with lots of bumps and wrong turns along the way.

Remembering: All around us there is evidence of how important remembering and memorial is to the human experience. Statues, funds, memorial events, and buildings abound. Why, then, are people afraid to speak the name of a deceased child to a bereaved parent? When someone has died, we long to keep their memory alive. Even more, we fear that they will be forgotten. I have found that people are eager to tell me about their losses when they realize that I am comfortable with the topic and interested in hearing about them.

Time: Time, by itself, will aid the healing process. But how that time is spent will make all the difference. Working through issues, making an effort to reinvest in life, taking a new, more fulfilling path in life will all hasten the healing process and help the wound to heal with a healthy and clean scar.

Getting help from community and religious organizations at a time of loss is a very hit and miss proposition. In some communities, information is readily available about where to go and whom to see. Other communities are lacking in available support. Mental health professionals are uneven in their ability to deal with traumatic losses, so care is recommended in choosing the right professional, if that is the desired course of action. As with anything else, recommendations from those you know are invaluable. Today, we are fortunate to have an enormous wealth of information and support services available on the Internet. With some careful searching, resources can be found there or will lead to the needed services in the community.